THE DEATH ROW ALL STARS

THE DEATH ROW ALL STARS

A Story of Baseball, Corruption, and Murder

HOWARD KAZANJIAN AND CHRIS ENSS

TWODOT®

GUILFORD, CONNECTICUT
HELENA, MONTANA
AN IMPRINT OF GLOBE PEQUOT PRESS

A · **TWODOT**® · **BOOK**

Project Editor: Lauren Brancato
Layout: Joanna Beyer

Library of Congress Cataloging-in-Publication data is available on file.

ISBN 978-0-7627-8756-2

Printed in the United States of America

For all those accused of crimes they did not commit

CONTENTS

ACKNOWLEDGMENTS

The trail used to research this book twisted and turned through countless libraries, newspaper offices, historical societies, museums, sheriffs' offices, prisons, and churches. We would like to thank the following people and organizations for their assistance in the preparation of this book:

Carl Hallberg, reference archivist at the Wyoming State Archives;

Duane Shillinger, author and historian in Rawlins, Wyoming;

Carol Reed at the Carbon County Museum Collections;

James E. Schmidt, investigator at the Uinta County Sheriff's Office;

Christopher Blue, outreach assistant at the Union Pacific Railroad Museum;

Lana Wilcox, county clerk and recorder in Evanston, Wyoming;

Lewis L. Gould, author and historian;

Dr. Marie Collins, historian for the Moroni Ewer family;

Rev. John Grabish, Sacred Heart of Jesus Parish in Allentown, Pennsylvania;

the staff at the Davenport Public Library in Davenport, Iowa; and

the South Dakota Archives Department.

A special note of appreciation is offered to Charles F. Seng for the background information he provided on Joseph Seng and to Olive Phelps for providing information about Alta Lloyd.

We are grateful to Barry Williams for his fact-checking expertise and to the editorial staff at Globe Pequot Press for their hard work and dedication.

Finally, we are sincerely indebted to our editor, Erin Turner, for giving us the opportunity to write about this historic happening.

FOREWORD

According to an article in the April 17, 1912, edition of the *Wyoming Tribune*, "No thrill equals that which comes when a home player sends the ball ringing off his bat safely to the outfield. As the number of bases gained by such a hit increases, so does the excitement mount. When one of those drives wins a game, its maker is a hero."

The American West of the early 1900s was the scene of great change. The transcontinental railroad cut a swath through the country, pulling the population away from the East, bringing progress to and signs of the coming industrial age. Boomtowns were turning into cities; the ways of the West were disappearing and giving way to the inevitable intrusion of change.

But as life became more sophisticated and industrial, a simple and pure game captured the attention of a nation. It would become a national pastime, but in Wyoming in 1910 baseball was an obsession.

Every town, every camp had leagues or teams of its own. Every team had stars who could easily play alongside Honus Wagner or Ty Cobb. But there were no baseball stars as unique as the Wyoming State Penitentiary Death Row All Stars of Rawlins, Wyoming.

And the star of the All Stars, Joseph Seng.

From the moment he arrived at the penitentiary, Seng was known more for his baseball prowess than his murder conviction. Within moments of his incarceration, prison officials got around to the task of creating a team and building a place to play.

The concept of prison reform and prisoner welfare was nonexistent in 1910. Time on the field was a precious escape from day-to-day life that could be both extremely hellish and (for some) lavishly privileged. Corruption and graft ran rampant. Prisoners were forced to work for little or no wages in the prison broom factory, denied basic necessities, fed rancid food, and forced to work road crews. Others were allowed to openly wander the streets of Rawlins, hunt rabbits outside the prison walls, and reap the monetary windfall of betting on the All Stars.

For the players, baseball was their life, their saving grace. Inside their cell, they were rapists, robbers, burglars, and thieves. But on the playing field, they were fast, hard, and possessed an inside fast ball no one could hit.

Primarily off the strength of Seng's arm (and his bat), the Death Row All Stars quickly became the talk of barrooms, brothels, and even political circles. Fortunes were being made by wagering in exchange for promises of time taken off their sentences and, for Seng, the possibility of a death penalty commutation.

For one cloudless Wyoming summer, residents of Rawlins boasted one of the finest baseball teams in the country. Scores of baseball fans came from all over the state, creating an abstract grandstand fan base. Socialites, merchants, and politicos sat alongside prospectors, ranchers, and drifters cheering for the men in the dark uniforms with "W-S-P" sewn on their chests.

The All Stars' exemplary play wasn't only the talk of the Wyoming territory but was lauded by sportswriters and fans as far away as New

York and Boston. Like the western heroes of dime novels, these felon players were indeed all stars.

But Seng's on-field performance failed to afford him great luxuries within the prison walls. For as many that respected and admired his abilities, there were those who resented his perceived celebrity status, making it their life's work to kill the prison right fielder.

Yet all of this seemingly left Seng unaffected. He was always a quiet gentleman. He spent his time off the field working alongside the prison doctor, writing letters to family and his spiritual advisor, and dreaming of the woman he loved—the woman whose husband's life he took, putting him behind bars, condemned to death.

On the field, he was alive and would continue to live. Joseph Seng was well aware that as long as the All Stars were on the field and generating money and fame for the prison and the state, he would be guaranteed to live another day. The conspiracy to keep the slugger alive reached from the guards and the warden to local officials and the governor himself.

Sadly, like everything around him, progress would greatly alter Seng's reality. Under the pressure of the growing morality (or guilt) of society, it was decided that the prisons needed to change. In order to save his own political hide, the governor vowed to end the wagering. Reading and writing were deemed more important to reforming prisoners than pitching and batting.

Before they were allowed to finish their inaugural season, the All Stars knew it was over.

Each player went back to his cell, back into his darkness. Some were paroled, some escaped, some died. But each one carried with him the memory of his time on the diamond, in the sunshine. They kept with them the absolute joy of the time in hell when they were allowed to play. They weren't playing for the glory, and certainly not for the money. They were playing for the love of the game; they were playing for the freedom.

They were playing for time.

—Skip Mahaffey, award-winning sports broadcaster,
talk show host, and author

INTRODUCTION

Walt Whitman once said, "I see great things in baseball." Convicted murderer Joseph Seng and other inmates on the Wyoming State Penitentiary baseball team saw great things in the game as well. Though they played only four games during the summer of 1911, the Death Row All Stars, as they were sometimes called, were one of the best and most respected ball clubs in the West. They had great incentive to do well at the game; these desperate men were led to believe that if they won they would receive lighter sentences or stays of execution.

From 1910 to 1919, one of the most eventful decades in baseball, many players associated with the professional clubs had reputations as hooligans and ruffians or worse. They were, according to baseball historian Bill James, a bunch of "shysters, con men, carpet baggers, drunks and outright thieves." These hard-bitten men might have fit right in with the convicts taking their turns at bat not for a salary or for the honor of their team but for survival. Culminating with the infamous Black Sox scandal of the 1919 World Series, it was a decade characterized by battles between players and owners, illegal gambling, and corruption in the national pastime.

Still, it was the national pastime, and nationwide the sport counted approximately fifty-six million fans. In rural states like Wyoming, the stands of small town stadiums in places like Rawlins were packed for games between the local teams. Across the United States men picked up bats and balls and spent their weekend afternoons and long summer weeknights on the diamond. The game got its start out west when Alexander Joy Cartwright, a bank clerk turned prospector, taught fellow forty-niners the game.[1] He organized a baseball club in San Francisco, and on February 22, 1860, the first game between Cartwright's club and a rival team in the area was played. Cartwright helped develop the game into the highly competitive sport in which the All Stars participated. He established the distance between bases at ninety feet, nine-person teams for nine innings, and three outs per team per inning. In addition to adding the position of shortstop, he eliminated the rule that allowed the defense to get a runner out by throwing the ball at him. He also divided the field into fair and foul territories.[2]

Praised for its logic and beauty, the sport of baseball was held in wide esteem nationwide. The December 12, 1906, edition of the *Atlantic Evening News* included this praise: "Baseball is the most logical form of athletic pastime evolved by man and the logical way to reform the despondent, down-trodden or devious. The game is the only one played which is founded upon exact and scientific lines. The playing field is laid out with such geometrical exactness, and with such close study of natural speed of foot and power of arm of the human animal as to give the defensive team an exactly equal chance with the attackers, and to compel both attacker and defender to approach the extreme limit of human speed and agility in every close play."

By the time the Wyoming prison baseball team took to the field in July 1911, more than sixty thousand clubs bringing together approximately seven hundred and fifty thousand men and boys over the age of twelve had been organized all over the United States. It seemed that practically everyone else in the country was a spectator.[3] And in many places throughout the country, spectators gathered to watch inmates take their turn in the batter's box or on the baseball field.

Concord Reformatory in Concord, Massachusetts, was the first institution to develop an organized sports program for inmates. In 1886 prison authorities at Concord organized several club and various sports teams as part of a movement they thought would offer practice in self-government. On Saturday afternoons the prisoner games included baseball, wrestling, and football. Neighboring towns frequently sent teams to play against the reformatory, and crowds gathered to watch.[4]

The introduction of prison athletics ushered in a new era in prison discipline. Organized sports made prison more tolerable for the inmates, offering an outlet for the dangers posed by the considerable downtime for prisoners. Prison authorities also regarded athletics as an opportunity to control the prisoners "in masses," and as a form of prison therapy, part of the "attempt to re-create the man in prison." The twin dynamics of control and rehabilitation, then, were built into the origins of prison recreational sports.[5]

While recreational sports were widespread in the US penitentiary system in the first half of the twentieth century, what made the baseball games the Death Row All Stars participated in different was that these men thought they were playing for their lives. The story of how the team came to be and how the community, the prison administration, and the prisoners themselves contributed to its demise is a tale of corruption, gambling, legal drama, and a fight for survival that resonates more than a hundred years later.

Even though their existence as a team was short, documentation about the Death Row All Stars, also known as Alston's All Stars, abounds. The *Washington Post* reported on the team's first game. Local newspapers reported on the team's efforts on the field—and told the stories of the men and their crimes. Still, finding information about the team and the players was difficult at times because names were often misspelled or spelled in a variety of ways. For example, George Saban's name was spelled three different ways in newspaper and historical accounts—Saban, Sabon, and Sabin. (His name is spelled Saban on the prison intake forms, and that is the spelling used throughout this book.)

The picture that emerges, however, after digging through archives and revisiting the scenes of the team's success, is that of a team that was fiercely proud of its skills and—for whatever reason—deeply devoted to winning. Regardless of the drama and controversy swirling around them in the prison, and regardless of their crimes, they were professionals on the field. And they were gentlemen. These men, criminals of all stripes, always tipped their hats to the loyal spectators, and for a brief time they rose above their offenses and dedicated themselves solely to the art of baseball.

CHAPTER ONE

A Fast Team

A blinding hot sun pushed its way out from behind a few clouds and stretched its rays across a baseball diamond above Overland Park in Rawlins, Wyoming, in the summer of 1911.[1] A crowd of people in the stands of the shade-free arena carved into the center of town waved cardboard fans in front of their faces in a futile attempt to push the merciless heat away from them. All eyes were trained on Thomas Cameron, the cherub-faced, overly tired pitcher who had the mound. He backhanded beads of sweat off his forehead as he stepped away from his position and looked over the fielders behind him.

Some of his teammates slapped their fists into their rough, well-worn gloves, and all shouted words of encouragement. Cameron adjusted his cap and pulled it down far over his forehead. He kicked the dirt under his feet, and a haze of powdery dry dust rose in the air around his ankles and settled on his grimy uniform. He stepped back onto the mound and readied himself to pitch. His arms rose high over his head as he started his windup. Rearing back on his left leg he fired a wild, high fastball. The alert batter turned away from the plate while fading backward to avoid the out-of-control pitch, but the ball ricocheted off his left shoulder and bounded into the stands.

A fat, unkempt umpire shouted for the batter to take his base as the spectators hissed at the rattled Cameron. The team captain, George Saban, stood near the dugout with a grim expression on his face. It was an unfortunate error. Cameron's shoulders sagged under the weight of what he knew could happen because of the mistake.

The team was warned that substantial bets had been placed on them to win the game. Influential leaders both in and out of the prison, including the warden, stood to benefit from a victory. That information came from the team captain and a prison guard. Individual errors that cost the team the win would result in death.

At the conclusion of the game, Cameron joined the other players on his team as they lined up single file along the third baseline. There wasn't a trace of satisfaction in the win or for a game well played on any of their faces. A half dozen burly, heavily armed guards carrying a long link of handcuffs and shackles approached the team. As the guards leveled their guns at the team, each player slipped the braces on and locked them in place.[2]

The Wyoming Supply Company Juniors, the team the convicts had just defeated, was known as one of the best teams in the state. They applauded and cheered the Wyoming State Penitentiary All Stars as they shuffled toward the exit of the stadium. The crowd followed suit, and the mesmerized onlookers watched the prisoners as they loaded onto the bus.[3] The players took their seats and peered back at the crowd through the barred windows.

Although the All Stars played the game of baseball with civility and respect, outside the sport their behavior was judged unruly and barbaric. Imprisoned for a variety of brutal crimes, some of which were worthy of the death penalty, these inmates had a gift for America's favorite pastime.[4]

━━◆━━

Thousands of men had transported heavy metal track into the Wyoming Territory in 1867, every spike driven into the earth that held the rails in place solidifying the Union Pacific Railroad's position in the region and bringing civilization to that part of the frontier. According to author and historian Francis B. Beard, "The Wyoming Territory was the child of the Union Pacific."[5] The railroad had plotted a course to the Pacific Ocean. The stops created along the way were based on accessibility to water or other important resources, such as coal, that were needed to keep the railroad engines moving along. Another objective the railroad had was to secure a share of cattle traffic. Towns the Union Pacific Railroad helped create had great economic promise.[6]

In Wyoming, Cheyenne, Laramie, Sheridan, and Rawlins became four popular rail towns. Ambitious businessmen descended upon the emerging hamlets, bought up parcels of land, and resold them to settlers eager to make a home for themselves in the territory.[7] Sandwiched between the Sierra Madre and Medicine Bow Mountains and the Haystack and Seminoe Mountains, Rawlins was founded in 1867 by John A. Rawlins, a decorated Civil War general and official sentry for the railroad.[8] The locale possessed fine drinking water, and after General Rawlins announced "it was the finest water he'd ever tasted," railroad executive Grenville M. Dodge, who was traveling with Rawlins and Rawlins's scouting party, declared that the site should be called Rawlins Springs. In time the name would be shortened to Rawlins.[9]

In spite of the trappings of civilization that came west with the railroad, Wyoming was still the Wild West in many ways. The safety of the early citizens of Rawlins depended upon the troops hired by the railroad to protect them. Native Americans angry over the presence of pioneers on their land tried to attack the town on several occasions. One such attempt was thwarted in June 1870. "Couriers came into Rawlins last night to report that soldiers had stopped a band of Sioux Indians from moving in on the establishment," the June 29, 1870, edition of the *New York Herald* read. "The confrontation took place twenty-five miles from Rawlins. There were two hundred Indians in number, fifteen were killed. No soldiers were hurt. Reinforcements and ammunition left Rawlins carried by lieutenants and scouts." By the end of the nineteenth century, however, the Wyoming Territory had largely evolved from a wild, undisciplined stretch of undeveloped West into a thriving, much-traveled-to state. Settlers of the big plains of Wyoming loudly sang praises of the territory's beauty the day the area was admitted to the Union in July 1890.[10] Prospectors came and extracted from the region's mountains rich deposits of coal and some gold, silver, and copper. Farmers sunk plows into the inhospitable earth and managed to grow a variety of crops. Businessmen opened hotels, banks, saloons, and mercantiles, and ranchers drove thousands upon thousands of herds of cattle over what many cattlemen believed to be the best grazing land in the nation.[11]

As the population of Wyoming increased, so did the crime rate. Authorities in individual towns across the state housed petty lawbreakers in local jails. Serious offenders were sent to a prison in Laramie. By the late 1880s, however, the facility at Laramie proved to be too small to accommodate all the convicts, and lawmakers began discussing where a new penitentiary could be constructed.[12] Rawlins had a reputation for dealing harshly with criminals. Desperados caught in the act of robbery, rape, or murder in the town were not only hanged, but sometimes actually skinned. Various items were made from the hides of these unfortunate lawbreakers, sold as souvenirs, and used as a warning to other would-be felons. Such was the case with George Parrott, alias Big Nose George, a gang member who attempted to rob a Union Pacific train.[13] After shooting and killing two Carbon County deputy sheriffs, he was lynched for the murders by Rawlins citizens in 1881 and shoes were made from his skin.[14]

Such dedication to seeing justice served made it easy for Wyoming's Ninth Legislative Assembly to agree that the best place to build the state penitentiary was Rawlins.[15] In 1888 state officials purchased land north of Rawlins from the Union Pacific Railroad Company, and construction on the penitentiary began. Rocks from the sandstone quarry south of town were used to build the prison. Holdups with legislative appropriations and poor weather conditions stalled building efforts over a fifteen-year period.[16]

Construction on the Wyoming State Penitentiary, affectionately known as the Crossbar Hotel, began in 1888. WYOMING STATE ARCHIVES, DEPT. OF STATE PARKS & CULTURAL RESOURCES

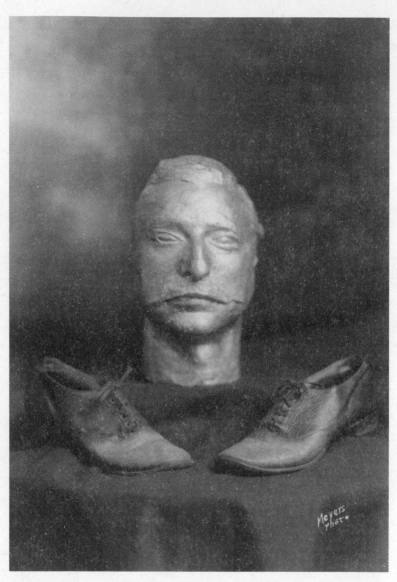

A plaster cast of "Big Nose" George Parrott's head and the shoes made from his skin. WYOMING STATE ARCHIVES, DEPT. OF STATE PARKS & CULTURAL RESOURCES

The December 16, 1896, edition of the Golden, Colorado, newspaper the *Colorado Transcript* informed readers that the new penitentiary building in Rawlins had been completed and that the governor, secretary of state, and state treasurer of Wyoming had inspected the finished product. "They found the work of the contractor performed in accordance with the terms of the contract made with him by the state," the article noted. "The new penitentiary will have to be furnished before the convicts can be transferred to it," the report concluded.

It would be five more years until the Wyoming State Penitentiary opened its doors to its first residents in 1901.[17] According to the December 14, 1901, edition of the *Rawlins Republican*, prisoners were transferred to the new structure on Thursday, December 12, 1901. The newspaper covered the momentous event in some detail:

> *The prisoners are being transported in a baggage car which has been fitted up for that purpose with cages for the guards in each end. The prisoners are shackled and handcuffed together. Benches are placed in the car for the men to sit upon.*
>
> *It is impossible to secure a sufficient number of shackles, so it was necessary to have a number of pairs made. These are riveted by a blacksmith after they are placed around the men's ankles and are cut off with a cold chisel after the men are delivered safely into the cell house of the new prison. The transfer is being affected without difficulty, and the authorities laugh at the sensational stories published in the Cheyenne and Laramie papers regarding an alleged plot to hold up and liberate some of the desperate ones.*
>
> *Several armed guards accompany each shipment. The second car load of fifty men arrived yesterday afternoon and another will be brought up tomorrow. There is considerable curiosity on the part of*

*the people to get a view of the men in stripes, but they seem to enjoy
the attention given them.*

*. . . The weather is quite cold for them in their ordinary prison
clothing, and they are no doubt glad when the prison walls again
protect them from the piercing winds. Better weather could not
have been chosen for the transfer, as no man no matter what his
opportunity would ever attempt to get away in weather like this.*

*In the first lot brought up were a number of the most desperate
characters, men serving long terms for murder and other crimes.
There will be two hundred two men held under confinement while
there are cell bunks for two hundred eight men in the Rawlins'
prison.*

The State Board of Charities and Reform appointed J. P. Hehn as
the first warden of the Wyoming State Penitentiary. Established by
the Wyoming State Legislature in 1890, the State Board of Charities
and Reform was responsible for all state reformatory and penal institutions "as the claims of the humanity and the public good require."[18]
Hehn, acting under the direction of the board and following practices
that were common all over the United States, put a convict leasing
program into place as one of the prison's standard practices.

The system of penal labor practices, referred to as lessee programs,
began in the southern United States. The convict leasing program provided prisoner labor to private parties. In the case of the Wyoming
State Penitentiary, millionaire Otto Gramm, a Laramie drugstore
owner, sheep rancher, railroad tie contractor, and mining speculator,
was the penitentiary's lessee.[19] Gramm provided work for the prisoners in a broom-making factory set up at the prison, and the state paid
his company for the convicts' daily support in the amount of fifty-
seven cents per prisoner per day.[20] The profits from the sale of the

brooms were intended to reduce the cost of the prison to the taxpayers, and having a leaseholder in place as part of the prison management was intended to lessen the administrative burden.[21] While the system achieved its economic goal, Gramm's reign as the head of the penitentiary lessee program was marred by accusations of abuse of the prisoners and malfeasance.[22] Corruption and lack of accountability were chief complaints about the lessee system nationwide.

The broom-making factory Gramm oversaw at the prison was called the Laramie Broom Company because it was originally run from the prison in Laramie. Several months after the Rawlins penitentiary was built, the company relocated to the new structure along with the inmates. Prisoners produced about sixty dozen brooms daily, not only constructing the brooms but also sorting the corn delivered by train that was to be used in the making of the different grades of brooms.[23]

Gramm had been embroiled in a scandal more than once in his career. While serving as state treasurer from 1888 to 1892, he was accused of misappropriation of funds. Although the money was eventually found, some prominent political leaders in Wyoming, including Governor Joseph Carey, questioned Gramm's integrity.[24] Gramm's time as the Wyoming State Penitentiary lessee was fraught with complaints from prisoners about neglect, and heated debates between Gramm and those who speculated that he and Warden Hehn personally benefitted financially from the program played out in the newspapers. Gramm was accused of skimping on provisions and medical care for inmates and pocketing a large percentage of the money given to him by the state to care for the prisoners.[25]

From the spring of 1903 until the summer of 1911, it is estimated the Ohio-born Gramm accumulated close to a quarter of a million dollars in revenue from the broom manufacturing operation at the prison. The finished products were shipped by train not only to hamlets within Wyoming, but also to Nebraska, California, Utah, Montana, Minnesota, South Dakota, Colorado, and Idaho. The price of brooms varied from $0.52 to $2.15 each.[26] Inmates were subjected to stiff penalties if quotas set by Gramm were not met. He rewarded guards who helped keep the system going with cash and made sure certain prisoners who helped keep the number of brooms produced high were provided with extra food or clothing.[27] According to historian T. A. Larson, Governor Carey vehemently condemned the state contract that enabled Gramm to add to his bank account with what amounted to free labor.[28] Much later, a report compiled by Wyoming state attorney Robert Murray revealed that the condemned "looked with distaste on the whole range of implications of the [lessee] contract."[29]

One of the objections to the program was that the labels affixed to the brooms did not identify the product as having been manufactured at the penitentiary, probably part of the prison's attempt to "skirt the contentious issue of free labor."[30] Prisoners often voiced their opinions about this dishonest behavior. Years after he was released, convict Harry A. Pendergraft wrote about the procedure. "The practice of that company of placing deceptive and misleading labels upon their products and similar questionable business methods of that nature were held up to the public as a menace to all honest free labor and to the great industries of the state."[31]

Pendergraft referred to conditions at the penitentiary under the rule of Warden Hehn and Otto Gramm as "a system of the dark ages." In a letter he wrote in the April 25, 1912, edition of the *Laramie Republican,* he claimed that Gramm and Hehn were "merciless" and that the penitentiary was an "incubator that breeds and nourishes criminal instincts and sends men from prison in a worse state of degradation than when they entered here." Other prisoners wrote that under Gramm's administration, tomato cans were used for drinking cups and meals were calculated down to the last bean so that just enough food was served to prevent starvation.[32]

State auditor Robert Forsyth and Charles Blydenburgh, leading members on the State Board of Charities and Reform, disagreed with the complaints about the prison administration. They insisted that Hehn and Gramm were adequately operating the facility with the least amount of taxpayer dollars.[33] Regardless of how well Forsyth, Blydenberg, Hehn, and Gramm believed the lessee system worked, a powerful opposition was about to eliminate Gramm's involvement in the program in spite of the influence of those who stood to benefit the most by keeping him in place.[34]

In April 1911, after more than a decade of being in operation, the lessee program was struck down by the Wyoming State Legislature.[35] Gramm, Forsyth, and Blydenberg were less than thrilled by the decision. Gramm and Warden Hehn's successor, Fred Hillenbrand, left their positions, and Governor Carey made Big Horn County sheriff Felix Alston the first state-appointed warden.[36]

Within days of Alston taking on the job, members of the State Board of Charities and Reform who disagreed with Gramm's ouster were questioning the new warden's ability to manage the prison. There were also questions surfacing about Governor Carey's honesty and his motives in removing Gramm and appointing Alston.[37] The issue of the governor's honesty had initially been brought up in 1895 by his political opponent for senate, Francis Warren, who accused Carey of being a "tax dodger."[38] Senator Warren, along with his supporters Forsyth and Gramm, implied that the governor and Alston saw the potential of financial gain for themselves at the penitentiary and in time would find their own way of exploiting the system.[39]

In spite of the backlash against his appointment, forty-six-year-old Alston was eager to begin work as warden of the Wyoming State Penitentiary. There were a number of programs, such as the lessee program, that he was pleased to see eliminated. He also wanted to introduce new opportunities, including physical fitness programs. Warden Alston also believed that inmates should give back to the community and began a program that put crews of prisoners to work making road repairs in the state.[40] The broom factory would remain a part of the prison's programs, but it would be managed by the prison administration and not as part of a lessee system.

Warden Alston's first months at the penitentiary were rocky. His plans for change were neither quickly nor easily embraced by either the inmates or the citizens of Rawlins. People in both groups refused to believe Warden Alston had the experience or ingenuity to be effective that his predecessor had possessed.[41] According to historical accounts found in the book *Annals of Wyoming*, prisoners began plotting their escape almost from the moment Warden Alston arrived on the scene.[42] He tried to reason with the inmates by agreeing to meet with those convicts who were considered leaders at the facility to address their concerns about him. But almost immediately he committed a grave error, by carelessly failing to invite an influential prisoner named Lorenzo Paseo to the summit.[43] Paseo took offense at the oversight and vowed to get the warden's attention and make him pay.

Irrespective of the turmoil, Warden Alston pressed on with reform at the prison. No change he instituted was as controversial inside or outside of the prison as the creation of an inmate baseball team.[44] Wyoming citizens, like people all over America, were enthusiastic about the sport. The entire town turned out to watch games, and the local ball field was another version of the town square, a place to be seen. It wasn't unusual for local businesses, politicians, and churches to sponsor teams of their own and to offer better jobs to the best players in order to keep them happy in the community.[45]

The front pages of the *Rawlins Republican*, the *Carbon County Journal*, and the *Cheyenne Daily Leader* covered in detail the winners and losers of the season's games between the Laramie Cowboys, the Cheyenne Indians, the Rawlins Team, the Rock Spring Ball Club, the Union Pacific Players, and the Green River Sluggers. Wyoming clubs also played games against teams in California, Arizona, and Utah.[46]

Warden Alston was an avid baseball fan, as were many of the inmates interred at the Wyoming State Penitentiary during a time when the entire country had been swept away by the sport. Shortstop Honus Wagner, center fielder Ty Cobb, and pitchers Christy Mathewson and Cy Young were the most well-known major league players of the time.[47] The 1911 season produced one of baseball's best rookie crops, led by Shoeless Joe Jackson, the only man to hit .400 as a rookie.

Fans cheered for players such as the Rawlins team pitcher "Slim Jim" Jenson and second baseman Jackie Weibrecht, and their on-field talents were the topics of much discussion.[48] An article from the September 21, 1911, edition of the *Rawlins Republican* noted that a preoccupation with baseball and a specific team's stars was a "cure for insanity." "Baseball dope, the batting averages, league standings, vital statistics, and the rest of the assorted, is first-aid to the curious and information is now being put to practical use in curling backward minds and incorrigible students in high school," the commentary read. "You may say without departing from the literal truth that baseball makes the insane sane." Doctor W. O. Kohn from the University of Illinois is quoted as saying "watching baseball and investing yourself emotionally in a game makes your mind as clear as glass."

Inmates at the Wyoming State Penitentiary received updates about their favorite major league baseball teams from family and friends. Oftentimes those letters would include newspaper clippings and post-cards with statistics and photographs of popular players. Members of the penitentiary baseball team would study the information and des-perately try to emulate their favorite athletes.

Warden Alston hoped the souls of players on the baseball team he organized would be uplifted by the game. The roster of inmate players he pulled together consisted of a dozen men ranging in age from nine-teen to thirty-eight, and their crimes were heinous. Shortstop Joseph Guzzardo had been convicted of manslaughter. Eugene Rowan, who played first base, and the catcher, James Powell, had both been con-victed of rape and attempted rape and attempted breaking and enter-ing. Sidney Potter, convicted of forgery, played center field. The left fielder, Earl Stone, and second baseman, Frank Fitzgerald, were both in for breaking and entering. Ora Carman, another left fielder, had been sentenced for grand larceny, as had third baseman John Crottie. Thomas Cameron, convicted of rape, was one of the team's pitchers; the backup pitcher, H. A. Pendergraft, had been convicted of grand larceny. George Saban, convicted of murder, was team captain, and Joseph Seng, also convicted of murder, alternated between playing catcher, shortstop, and right field.[49]

On Monday, July 24, 1911, the front page of the *Washington Post* ran a story about the Wyoming State Penitentiary's newly formed ball club and their first game. The story centered on the player that helped the penitentiary team to their first win. "With a murderer condemned to death as the right fielder, and other members of the opposing team convicts, the Wyoming Supply Company ball club put up a classy game against the Alstons, losing, however by the score of eleven to one," the article touted. "Joseph Seng, right fielder for the Alstons, is under sentence to be hanged. Seng made two home run hits over the penitentiary wall. One of his hits cleared the bases bringing in three others and scoring himself."

Warden Alston's critics were keeping a watchful eye on his reforms—and especially on the baseball team. Warden Alston would come to realize that the task at hand was even more contentious and daunting than expected.

CHAPTER TWO

The Captain and the Critic

Sheep rancher Joe Emge woke up fast from a fitful slumber late on a chilly night in early April 1909 near Spring Creek, Wyoming. There was no light inside the wagon where he and one of his ranch hands had bedded down. When the darkness around him began to break up, he saw the dim, blurred outline of a man standing over him. Joe strained to focus on the object the imposing figure was pointing at him. When he realized the object was a six-shooter, it was too late.[1]

Cattleman George Saban pulled the trigger back on his .35 automatic and fired a shot into Joe's face. He quickly pulled the trigger back again and slapped the hammer with his left hand; it was the fastest way to get off several more shots. His objective was to kill not only Joe but also the other man in the wagon. It was a job the gunman dispatched with ease and no regret.[2]

Saban jumped out of the vehicle and stood in a pool of light cast by a smoldering campfire. He heard gunfire erupting inside a second wagon close by, and he turned to see what had happened.[3]

Joe Allemand, a sheep rancher with a bullet hole in his back, stumbled out of the second wagon, picked himself up, and staggered away from the scene, his hands in the air. Two more gunmen, Herb Brink and Ed Eaton, stepped out of the wagon behind him. Herb leveled his Winchester at Joe and fired. Joe lurched forward and fell hard in the dirt, dead. "It's a hell of a time at night to come out with your hands up," Herb quipped.[4]

Herb marched over to a stand of sagebrush, snapped off a branch, and lit it from the campfire. The brush crackled and snapped as it burned. He held it up in the air and watched the flame grow, then tossed it under the wagon nearest him. In a matter of moments the vehicle was engulfed in fire. George followed Herb's lead, grabbing dry vegetation and fueling the flames licking the wheels of the wagon.[5]

As the three men watched the fire burn and consume the vehicles and the gear around them, they heard the report of another series of gunshots in the near distance. Four of George and Herb's cohorts had unloaded their weapons into a large herd of sheep. The few animals that managed to escape scattered, bleating loudly as they ran away.[6]

George walked over to his horse, which was tied to an old, rain-bleached post, and lifted himself into the saddle as though he hadn't a care in the world. He nudged his ride away from the chaos and trotted off into the shadows of the landscape, leaving the others to follow after him.[7]

On April 3, 1909, Felix Alston, then the Big Horn County sheriff, arrived at the scene with a few deputies in tow. He found Allemand's body lying near the smoldering embers of his wagon with one of his sheep dog's puppies curled up on his chest. The burned bodies of Emge and his ranch hand were among the charred vehicles as well.[8]

The brutal murders were the product of an ongoing feud between Wyoming cattlemen and sheep ranchers over the use of rangeland

A number of popular saloons and gambling dens lined Front Street in Rawlins, Wyoming, in 1911. WYOMING STATE ARCHIVES, DEPT. OF STATE PARKS & CULTURAL RESOURCES

grass. Cattle owners had long shown their intolerance for the encroaching wave of sheepmen eager to take advantage of the opportunities of the open range. The cattlemen claimed the land was for their specific use based on land-use terms drawn up in territorial days. Anyone who challenged the cattle ranchers' claims to their proprietary use of the resources of the plains was dealt with harshly.[9]

Scenes such as the one that Sheriff Alston was investigating that April morning were all too common. And justice for the perpetrators was all too rare, partly because they were often some of the most influential men in the area. "We know who some of the participants were, but had no bona fide evidence," Alston wrote in his memoirs. "There are many depredations committed against the sheepmen. Thousands of sheep killed and left to rot on the plains, a number of sheepherders murdered."[10]

Seven men, all prominent Big Horn County stockmen, were eventually arrested for the crime and were placed on trial in mid-October 1909.[11] According to the October 19, 1909, edition of the Montana newspaper the *Anaconda Standard,* the arrests of the men came as the result of "an investigation started by the Wyoming Wool Growers Association." Members of the Wool Growers Association had little trust in the efforts of county officials. Many of those officials were cattlemen, and the association doubted that the region's law enforcement agents could perform their duties in an unbiased manner.[12] That doubt extended to Sheriff Alston, who himself had come to Wyoming in 1892 in search of a "new and more fruitful range for his cattle."[13] The Wyoming Wool Growers Association initially hired Pinkerton detective Joe LeFlores to investigate the Spring Creek Raid, but ultimately it was Sheriff Alston who apprehended the killers, including George Saban.[14]

Even after an escape attempt was thwarted while the perpetrators were on bail awaiting trial, the accused were still convinced that the

Felix Alston served as penitentiary warden from 1911 to 1919.   WYOMING
STATE ARCHIVES, DEPT. OF STATE PARKS & CULTURAL RESOURCES

cases against them would be dropped because sheep raiders were generally not prosecuted, but a jury found them guilty of murder.[15] Saban was sentenced to more than twenty years in prison and was ordered to serve his time at the state penitentiary in Rawlins.[16]

Fifteen months after Saban began serving his sentence, Alston, the sheriff responsible for his arrest, was hired on as the warden of the facility.[17] In May 1911, when Warden Alston formed the penitentiary baseball club, he made Saban the team captain.[18] Historian Duane Shillinger speculates that the State Board of Charities and Reform pressured Warden Alston to give Saban special treatment in prison—including letting him participate in a work release program and play on the baseball team. Many prominent cattlemen and politicians, after all, viewed his crimes as necessary for the survival of cattle ranching. There may have been another reason as well. According to the warden's grandson, Scott Alston, Saban, a longtime neighbor of the Alstons and a guest at Felix's 1900 wedding, was the warden's closest friend.

Otto Gramm was suspicious of the influence cattlemen had on the State Board of Charities and Reform and on Warden Alston. Still irritated by Governor Joseph Carey's decision to terminate his role with the lessee program, Gramm paid close attention to the situation at the prison in hopes of acquiring evidence of wrongdoing and using the knowledge as leverage to reinstate the lessee program and get himself reappointed head of the profitable venture.[19]

By June 1911 Gramm had begun the process of transferring the duties of running the Laramie Broom Company to L. W. Senville.[20] The lessee program had ended, and rumors of reform permeated the cells and mess hall at the penitentiary. Inmates discussed the need for better food, uniforms, and both recreational and educational programs.[21] Articles in the penitentiary newsletter addressed inmates' concerns about how law-abiding citizens would react to convicts participating

Inmate #1441 George Saban, Team Manager. WYOMING STATE ARCHIVES, DEPT. OF STATE PARKS & CULTURAL RESOURCES

in activities that would take them off prison grounds for a time. Who George Saban and Warden Alston would select for the baseball team and when the team would be ready for a game, and whether the public would accept them, were other topics of great speculation.[22]

Saban had been in prison more than a year, awaiting an answer on an appeal to overturn his conviction on the grounds that his guilty plea had been obtained under duress, when Warden Alston enlisted his leadership skills for the baseball team. If not for Saban's physical challenges (two of the fingers on his left hand had been amputated at the second joint, and two fingers on his right hand had been amputated at the third joint), he might have been an exceptional player and not just the team captain.[23] But he was a logical choice for captain nonetheless, as the respect Saban had among many of the cattlemen in the community was shared by the inmates at the penitentiary. He was considered by his partners in crime as an old cowman, well suited for the job of attacking sheepherders who dared bring their animals into the cattle region.[24] Some prison guards and prison officials felt the same way about him.

Saban was one of the prisoners assigned to road improvement work. Guards daily led the inmate work crew to sections of roads in Rawlins that needed to be repaired and escorted them back to their cells in the evenings. Because several guards, whose families were in the cattle business, believed his actions against the sheepherders were justified and the sentence imposed too harsh, Saban was allowed to leave the detail dressed in civilian clothing and frequent popular gambling dens when he pleased.[25]

Warden Alston was hopeful that his prison ball club would be received as the hometown favorite. Patrons of gambling parlors along the South Front–East Fifth Street railroad crossing in Rawlins looked forward to the day when the team was organized. The earlier the oddsmakers could evaluate the players, the better idea they had about how much to wager on the team. Customers who frequented establishments such as Wolf's, the Senates, the Elkhorn, and the Alhambra followed the baseball clubs that came up against the Rawlins team, scrutinized their weaknesses and strengths, and bet appropriately.[26] And some of them may have had inside information from prisoner and team captain George Saban.

CHAPTER THREE

Outlaw in the Infield

Few spectators would have bet against Joseph Seng when he was catching for All Stars pitcher Thomas Cameron.[1] Cameron, a twenty-year-old coal miner and native of Tennessee, had a terrific fastball and was a good hitter.[2] Seng, the standout performer on the team, signaled the talented pitcher on what throw to use. Under Seng's direction Cameron struck out the majority of batters that faced him.[3]

Born in Allentown, Pennsylvania, in 1882, Seng came from a large German family.[4] His father, Anthony Seng, was a proud man who had been born in Baden, Germany. He moved to the United States with his parents in 1878 and married Anna Sapple in the Sacred Heart of Jesus Parish in 1880. All of Anthony and Anna's children were christened at the parish.[5] Just before the turn of the century, Joseph Seng had been a laborer at one of the textile mills in the area. From 1903 to 1908 he resided in New York, and some history records indicate he worked for a prominent railroad line as a detective.[6] Then, after a brief

The Union Pacific Railroad was the leading employer in Wyoming in the 1900s. WYOMING STATE ARCHIVES, DEPT. OF STATE PARKS & CULTURAL RESOURCES

visit with his parents in Allentown in the summer of 1908, the twenty-six-year-old Seng departed for points west.[7]

Baseball had always been part of Seng's life. According to notes made by his spiritual advisor, Rev. Peter Masson of the Sacred Heart of Jesus Parish in Allentown, Joseph had a "natural aptitude for baseball, but never displayed ambition for much else." Still, he didn't appear to be much of a troublemaker. In fact, the brown-haired, blue-eyed Seng was a diminutive five-foot-five and was said to have a very moderate temper.[8] "He never shied away from long hours on the job," Rev. Masson continued, "and was mindful to give an employer all that was required of him and then some."

After Seng stepped off the train in Rawlins, Wyoming, in July 1908, he walked to one of the saloons just beyond the railroad tracks. Rev. Masson's notes about the letters he received from Seng painted a picture of his visit to the saloon:

When he entered the business he heard the sound of chips clinking from a side room. A bartender was behind the bar pouring drinks. Patrons were scattered about talking and laughing. Joseph found a spot at a table and sat down. He ordered something to drink while studying the "help wanted" section of a newspaper left behind on the chair next to him.

Customers filtered in and out of the establishment, some exchanged a word or two with a couple of men near the bar. Before walking away from the men the patrons handed them money. Like many saloons throughout the West, gamblers had staked out their territory and were enticing people to wager on boxing and wrestling matches, horse races and political races.[9]

A reading of the *Rawlins Republican* between May and June 1908 might have led to the conclusion that there was wide interest in stamping out vice in the region—or at least regulating it for the better of the community. In fact, gambling had been outlawed statewide in 1902, but in many communities, it was still widely accepted and officials followed a strict policy of pretending not to notice the poker games and bookmakers in local saloons. The *Rawlins Republican* revealed the ambivalence about the prohibition of gambling and prostitution. "This paper is opposed to gambling," a May 13, 1908, editorial read.

Nothing can be said in its favor; but we can't approve of the action of the county authorities in putting the lid on it just at this time. In as much as it was prompted by a desire to get even with a few who opposed them in the primaries, had this action been taken months ago it could have been defeated. Coming at this time all thinking people will understand its political significance.

The county and prosecuting attorney, disgruntled by defeat at the last election, have taken it upon themselves to try and rid certain sections of the city of gambling and deplete the treasury to the tune of over twelve thousand dollars a year, to say nothing of the individual losses the program will entail. As a consequence public improvements so far as the city is concerned will have to be discontinued; expenses will have to be cut in almost every conceivable way, and the great majority of our merchants will experience a sudden and serious decline in business. . . .

So far as the inmates of houses of prostitution are concerned they should be regulated and that is all. The highest practical civilizations on earth recognize such institutions as necessary evils and it is possible that great harm [to the economy] will result if these people are forced to leave the city.

This newspaper is opposed to gambling but do not favor its abolition at this time. We do not believe that gambling should be made a political issue. . . . From a monetary point of view gambling is a good thing for Rawlins—it puts money in the treasury and improves the city. Consequently, since those who gamble are not necessarily heads of families and have only themselves to look out for, and since those who gamble will gamble regardless . . . we can't see why the city and its individual enterprises should suffer.[10]

According to the July 20, 1908, edition of the *Carbon County Journal*, "residents throughout Wyoming challenged the law as unconstitutional" and noted that the "penalty provided [which was sometimes five to ten years in prison] was excessive and inhumane."

According to Rev. Masson, Seng absorbed the scene in the saloon as a few more eager individuals conducted gambling business with the men at the end of the bar, and then he went on his way. After the brief stop in Rawlins, Seng traveled more than two hundred miles west to the town of Evanston in Uinta County, near the Utah border.[11] In Evanston, Seng rented a room from a lodger named Moroni Ewer, who was also of German extraction and was originally from Pennsylvania. The fifty-five-year-old Ewer worked for the Union Pacific Railroad as a laborer and was married with two children.[12]

The town of Evanston was bustling due to the influence of the railroad—Evanston was "the end of the tracks." The Union Pacific Railroad machine shop and roundhouse was located just outside of town. The facility offered a convenient location for steam locomotives to fill up on coal and water. The roundhouse was used to service locomotives. The massive circular workstation featured a turntable that enabled access to engines and cars being stored or repaired. The roundhouse and machine shop combined employed 125 people, and the railroad line was always in need of new workers.[13] Seng was hired on as a watchman, perhaps because of his earlier experience in New York.[14]

At the end of a long workday, Seng and the other railroad agents would have flocked to the gaming houses that were just as abundant in Evanston as they were in Rawlins. Some politicians and some community members wanted the houses shut down because they believed that gambling was immoral, degraded communities, and led to violent crime. However, some prominent public figures such as Governor Joseph Carey were rumored to have enjoyed placing wagers on horses.[15] In fact, he raised racehorses on his twenty-one-thousand acre CY Ranch south of Fort Casper with his brothers, Dr. John Carey and R. Davis Carey.

The brothers ran forty thousand head of cattle and five hundred head of horses on their spread, and C-Y Ranch horses participated in endurance races from Evanston, Wyoming, to Denver, Colorado.[16] Governor Carey's peers, believing he had a history of betting on the races, felt he was being hypocritical by opting to enforce antigambling laws.[17]

Political leaders with an eye toward putting an end to major offenses driven by gambling went as far as shutting down gambling operations throughout communities to curtail the activity. In early June 1908 the town of Rock Springs, Wyoming, was ordered "closed" by law enforcement. According to the June 13, 1908, edition of the Rock Springs newspaper *The Journal,* "not only are all of the regular gambling places closed, but all slot machines, merchandise and other wise, have been stopped." Gaming establishments in other Wyoming locales such as Hulette were raided by state officials and the gambling tables burned. Roulette tables, faro layouts, twenty-one tables, and other gambling paraphernalia were used as fuel to start the bonfire.[18] Nothing seemed to stop the spread of the activity.

Seng had more on his mind than gambling as he established his new life in Evanston. When he arrived for his first day at work for the Union Pacific Railroad, "the first thing he noticed was a crude baseball field just beyond the massive building that housed several engines in various stages of repair. . . . The four acres of ball field was like an oasis in the midst of scraps of metal and tools, and locomotives belching smoke. The turf was a mixture of dust and weeds and the path from one base to the next was well traveled."[19]

Seng walked through an organized maze of railroad track and cars until he reached the main office, where the duties of his job as watchman were explained to him by his supervisor William Lloyd. Lloyd, a twenty-seven-year-old man from Davenport, Iowa, was a detective for the Union Pacific Railroad.[20] According to Christopher Blue, a

The Union Pacific Roundhouse in Evanston, Wyoming, where Joseph Seng and William Lloyd were employed. COURTESY OF THE EVANSTON URBAN RENEWED AGENCY

historian at the Union Pacific Railroad Museum, Seng's job entailed "patrolling railroad yards, cars, and stations or other facilities to protect the company property or shipments and to maintain order." He was also responsible for "apprehending or removing trespassers or thieves from railroad property or coordinating with law enforcement agencies in the apprehension or removal of trespassers or thieves."[21]

Six months prior to Seng's move to Wyoming, a series of cargo thefts had been perpetrated on the Union Pacific line that ran from Carbon County, Wyoming, to Weber County, Utah.[22] Lloyd, whose job was to investigate any crimes committed on railroad property, had been working on the case and his investigation had led him to a man named Toy Smith. Smith had a long list of previous offenses to his credit, and Lloyd was certain he was guilty of stealing from the railroad. Seng's arrival and hiring on as night watchman freed Lloyd to pursue Smith, a reported opium addict who had attempted to shoot Union Pacific Railroad agents on his trail. After quickly training Seng on all that his job entailed, Lloyd left Evanston to join in the search for Smith.[23] The agents eventually caught the crook outside Ogden, Utah, and arrested him.[24]

Lloyd's role as investigator for the Union Pacific meant quite a lot of time spent away from his wife, Alta, a twenty-four-year-old born and raised in South Dakota. His absences had taken a toll on their marriage. The couple had wed in Rapid City, South Dakota, in June 1908 and had moved to Evanston late that same year. They had no children, and Alta felt that her husband was too preoccupied with his job and had lost interest in her. Seng met the lonely Mrs. Lloyd when she visited the Union Pacific Railroad roundhouse to inquire after her husband. She worried about him when he was gone from home because of work. At some point after their meeting, Seng and Alta became romantically involved.[25]

According to Alta's great-great-niece, Olive Phelps, Alta often visited Emma Ewer, wife of Moroni Ewer, an employee of the Union Pacific Railroad and the innkeeper who rented a room to Joseph Seng. It was during these visits that Seng and Alta had a chance to pursue their feelings for one another.[26] William Lloyd remained seemingly unaware of his wife's relationship with Seng. Occasionally, the Ewers, their two children, Alta, Seng, and an unsuspecting William would travel the three hours to Rawlins to watch the Rawlins baseball team play. The last game they all attended together was on Sunday, July 17, 1910, and the Rawlins ball club demonstrated its superiority over a team from Saratoga, winning the game by a score of eleven to four.[27]

Alta's family suspects that William became aware of his wife's infidelity not long after the outing to Rawlins in July 1910. "I only know what my mother had to say about the situation," Olive Phelps noted. "Alta and William were fighting a lot, and given everything the newspapers reported after the fact, we just figured he found out that Joseph Seng was the other man."[28]

The August 6, 1910, edition of the *Laramie Republican* reported that on August 4, 1910, witnesses overheard William Lloyd, Alta Lloyd, and Joseph Seng arguing loudly around seven o'clock at night near a park in Evanston. Witnesses saw the two men squaring off for a fight. Lloyd appeared to be the aggressor, and Seng was standing his ground. Alta stood next to her husband and was apparently interjecting her own thoughts into the heated discussion when Seng suddenly stepped to one side, reached into the breast pocket of his jacket, and removed a gun.

The *Republican* reported that Joseph then fired a shot, and William fell to the ground. "Mrs. Lloyd stumbled over her husband's prostrate form and while she was leaning over his body Joseph fired two shots," the article continued.

Immediately following the shooting of his former employer, Joseph emptied the remaining three shots of his .41 Colt revolver into the ground, and a throng gathered on the scene. Joseph did not appear excited and told a bystander to inform an officer, warning others to keep away from him. Special city officer James Downs was soon on the grounds and Joseph immediately gave himself up to that officer. His only explanation of the tragedy was "I beat him to it," meaning that Lloyd had attempted to pull his gun first. In this statement it is said that the prisoner is both corroborated and contradicted by witnesses. Joseph was placed in jail and is said to have been cool and collected at all times.

Detective Lloyd had just returned from Ogden, where he was summoned as a witness in the Toy Smith case. He was on his way to attend a street carnival with his wife when Joseph joined the pair and together they walked down the fatal path. When Lloyd's body was picked up his revolver was found by his side. Joseph is in jail.

Mrs. Lloyd's screams were pathetic at the sound of the first shot, and she became hysterical at the sight of her wounded husband as she lay at his feet. The wounded man was carried to his private [railroad] car, where he survived for thirty minutes after being shot.

News of the murder spread quickly. An article in the August 6, 1910, edition of the *Atlantic Evening News* noted that "while walking along a street with his wife, William Lloyd, traveling detective for the Union Pacific, was shot instantly and killed by Joseph Seng. Seng had been discharged by Lloyd and investigators on the case say that was the reason he was murdered. Seng denies the allegation insisting that his actions were in self-defense." The August 26, 1910, edition of the *Casper Press* reported that "William Lloyd, assistant special agent for the Union Pacific, was shot and killed last Thursday night by Joseph Seng."

According to the September 14, 1910, edition of the *Cheyenne State Leader*, Seng was arraigned in the district court in Evanston on a charge of murder in the first degree, to which he entered a plea of not guilty. His attorneys had the case continued to April 1911. "The state had also succeeded in getting an unusual order from the court," the article elaborated. "Twenty-four state's witnesses on motion of the prosecuting attorney have been placed under heavy bond to appear for the trial."

Seng was held at the Uinta County jail throughout the winter of 1910–11. His case went to trial in April 1911. Public opinion and the

Inside the Wyoming State Penitentiary. COURTESY OF THE WYOMING STATE ARCHIVES
DEPARTMENT #26033

press seemed to be against him. According to the April 8, 1911, edition of the *Wyoming Press*, "the prosecution had more than a dozen witnesses, all of them leading to the supposition that Joseph would be convicted and hanged for the most atrocious murder to happen in Evanston, Wyoming, in years. . . . One shot pierced William Lloyd's right ear and came out at the side of the nose," the newspaper reported. "The second entered in front of the left ear and came out the corner of the eye."

Alta Lloyd's relatives believe she must have been in a state of shock over the violent incident. "We have no information that she spoke of the killing until after Joseph Seng was convicted," Olive Phelps stated. "It's assumed that she felt incredibly guilty over the crime."[29] Seng never denied firing on William Lloyd but insisted he acted in self-defense. The only defense he gave at his hearing, however, was "I beat him to it." A witness by the name of H. R. McGee testified that he saw the gun Lloyd was carrying fall out his pocket when he dropped to his knees after being shot.[30]

At the conclusion of the highly publicized proceedings, on April 13, 1911, Seng was convicted of murder in first degree and his sentence was set down by Judge D. H. Craig. "It is therefore considered, ordered and decreed by the court," the *Wyoming Press* quoted Judge Craig as saying, "that Joseph Seng be transported to the state penitentiary and that before sunrise on the 22nd of August be hanged by the neck until dead."[31]

CHAPTER FOUR

Home at the Crossbar Hotel

The sheriff of Uinta County delivered Joseph Seng to the state penitentiary on April 18, 1911.[1] An endless blue sky was the backdrop for the massive, three-story structure that day. High, barbed wire fence lined the building on all sides, and a plaque on the structure read Welcome to the Crossbar Hotel. Felix Alston, who had taken over the duties of prison warden the day before, watched Seng arrive. A pair of guards helped the shackled and handcuffed prisoner out of the vehicle in which he was transferred. The iron-barred door in front was opened, and Seng was escorted inside the penitentiary. The doors were then closed and locked behind him.[2]

According to Joseph Seng's family, his father, Anthony, had cried when he read an article about his son in the April 22, 1911, edition of the *Wyoming Press*. "On last Monday morning Sheriff Ward and Special Deputy Sam Rider took Joseph Seng, the convicted murderer of William Lloyd, to the penitentiary where the man will be confined until he is executed," the report announced. "Seng was handcuffed to

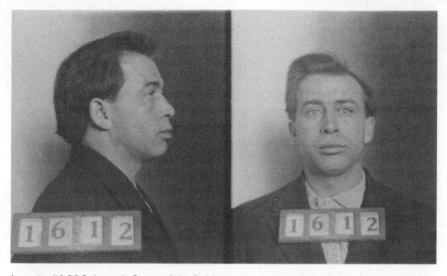

Inmate #1612 Joseph Seng, right fielder. WYOMING STATE ARCHIVES, DEPT. OF STATE PARKS & CULTURAL RESOURCES

Sheriff Ward . . . he passed through the streets of Evanston thus man-acled; he was smoking a cigar, and was accompanied by his customary indifference as to the gravity of the situation."

There was a standard routine for admitting an inmate into a state facility. The guards would lead a prisoner into an intake room and remove his shackles and chains. They would remove all items from the prisoner's pockets and set them aside on a table to be inventoried. The prisoner was then ordered to remove his clothes. A guard carry-ing a fire hose would enter the intake room and point the hose at the prisoner. When the water was flipped on, the force generally slammed the prisoner back against the stone wall. After a few moments the water was shut off, and the guards would pull the prisoner to his feet. A huge scoop of delousing powder was then tossed on him. Gasping and coughing, blinking powder from his eyes, the prisoner was then shoved toward a trustee cage, a small, defined area where the "trustee," an inmate who had proven himself trustworthy and had been given a job within the prison, was separated from the prisoner by a thick wall of wire rope with a small slot in it.[3]

The trustee would slide a short stack of items through the slot—prison clothes and a Bible. A doctor would be called in to give the prisoner a cursory examination. He would inspect every part of the prisoner's body, making note of every scar, tattoo, and birthmark. Joseph Seng had a tattoo on his left forearm of an American shield and eagle and a banner with the word Union written inside it; a tattoo of a butterfly, four aces, and a pair of dice on his right forearm; and a large spot scar above his left wrist and on his right knee. After the doctor completed the exam, the guards would lead the prisoner out of the room clutching his belongings against his bare chest.[4]

All prisoners were asked a series of standard questions, including their religion, how much schooling they'd had, habits of life, and special skills. Seng was asked about his occupation during the intake process, and the guard on duty listed him as a ribbon weaver on the convict form.[5] Somehow it was also noted that Seng was particularly skilled at baseball. Warden Alston and George Saban would be made aware of the new inmate's ability.

It was coincidence that Seng's tenure at the facility started at roughly the same time as Alston's. Alston's ascendance to the role of warden (and Otto Gramm's ouster) was front-page news across the state. Governor Carey, along with several state newspapers, referred to Alston as "the most remarkable criminal catcher of Wyoming."[6] Readers were reminded of Alston's storied career in law enforcement, including his 1908 capture of a notorious horse thief named R. L. Stratton. "Sheriff Felix Alston has a reputation among peace officers and criminals of never quitting a trail. No man he ever undertook to run down has escaped," read a contemporary account in the *Big Horn*

Otto Gramm ran the controversial lessee program at the penitentiary for more than seven years. WYOMING STATE ARCHIVES, DEPT. OF STATE PARKS & CULTURAL RESOURCES

County Rustler. "His detective operations led him into every state of the Rocky Mountains and to many outside that area. He seems to possess a psychic instinct for locating criminals."[7]

The April 19, 1911, edition of the *Cheyenne State Leader* not only echoed previous praise for the lawman, but also applauded Governor Carey's decision to oust Gramm from his role in the prison. "Speaking of contrast," the article began, "think of the difference in caliber of Otto Gramm, retiring manager of the state penitentiary, and Felix Alston, the incoming manager."

Gramm was, to all appearances, still a very influential member of the Wyoming community. He was a member of the public school board, president of the Board of Trustees for the University of Wyoming, a probate judge, and Albany County treasurer.[8] However, not long after terminating his contract with the penitentiary, Governor Carey demanded Gramm's resignation from the university board.[9] According to the April 21, 1911, edition of the *Nevada State Journal*, Gramm initially refused the directive and challenged the governor to issue charges to remove him. "Gramm was an issue in the last political campaign being the Albany County member of the Republican state convention and vice-chairman of the convention," the article explained. "He has been a member of the board of trustees of the university for sixteen years, being first appointed in 1895."

In spite of his conflict with the governor, Gramm still had very powerful friends—and he had decided to make Alston his enemy. Gramm and a few members of the State Board of Charities and Reform believed Governor Carey had taken a big gamble when he appointed Alston as superintendent of the state penitentiary at Rawlins.[10] Senator Francis Warren was one of Gramm's most powerful allies.[11] They shared a common enemy in Governor Carey and in his close associate, Alston. Any progress Governor Carey and Warden Alston hoped to

Senator Francis E. Warren was a staunch opponent of Governor Joseph Carey and critic of Warden Alston. WYOMING STATE ARCHIVES, DEPT. OF STATE PARKS & CULTURAL RESOURCES

make at the state penitentiary was met with opposition from Gramm and subsequently his champion, Senator Warren.

Warden Alston and Governor Carey agreed that the transition from the old guard to the new would be a struggle, but Alston was determined to overcome the initial setbacks that went along with the job. He would earn $2,500 a year to run the institution, secure the public safety, and manage the replacement of the lessee system with a state-run operation.[12] "The manner in which this institution has been conducted has been a disgrace to the state," Governor Carey announced to his constituents in early 1911. "I believe that where practicable, the convicts, who are sufficiently reliable, should be given work on public highways in the open air and that others should be given work inside the penitentiary, there should be definitive rules for the inmates, that includes steady work for which they need palatable and healthful food."[13]

In less than two months of Alston being on the job, however, problems at the prison were mounting. A guard had been killed and three convicts had escaped. The June 2, 1911, edition of the *Carbon County Journal* reported that inmates kidnapped a guard and made a clean getaway. "Yesterday afternoon occurred one of the most unlooked and unique escapes from the penitentiary that ever occurred in the state," the article read. "Three prisoners and a guard left for Coal Gulch with a load of coal and shale. When they had not returned by one o'clock in the afternoon the warden investigated and found no trace of the team, the men or the guard." One of the convicts with the guard in tow eventually gave himself up to the authorities. The other two escaped prisoners were never found.

The incident generated a lot of publicity and left the community worried about the possibility of repeat episodes. Historian and author Lewis Gould and Duane Shillinger suspects the problems were

Governor Joseph Carey denied a stay of execution for convicted murderer and baseball player Joseph Seng. WYOMING STATE ARCHIVES, DEPT. OF STATE PARKS & CULTURAL RESOURCES

exacerbated by disgruntled public officials such as Gramm.[14] Under-mining prison operations would have strengthened the argument that his lessee program was necessary to maintain order. Gramm was convinced that inmates, by nature of the fact that they were convicted felons, needed a stern hand to guide them through until they were released. Publicly, and perhaps a bit disingenuously, he objected to any privileges being extended to prisoners, believing that any such privileges would be exploited by the inmates and by those in charge of the system.[15] Alston's scheme to form a baseball team at the prison particularly rankled.

Shortly after the arrivals of Joseph Seng and Felix Alston at the Wyoming State Penitentiary, plans for the team began to fall into place. Alston's All Stars practiced on a regulation-size field in the exercise yard surrounded by a massive stone wall. Armed guards watched the team run the bases from a glass-enclosed tower. During regular visits to the prison to transfer oversight of the broom-making process, Otto Gramm watched the team, too.[16]

CHAPTER FIVE

Path to Righteousness

It was evident after practicing with the other men on the team only a short while that Joseph Seng was an exceptional baseball player. News of the talented addition to Alston's All Stars spread quickly throughout the area. Patrons who frequented the Turf Exchange, the Senate, the Elkhorn, and other watering holes in Rawlins speculated on how well the team would do against more established ball clubs in the region.[1] George Saban encouraged such talk whenever he made stops at the saloons as part of his duties transporting items to and from the prison accompanied by prison guard D. O. Johnson in the penitentiary wagon. Security was always lax where Saban was concerned. He came and went from tavern to tavern as he pleased and boasted about the baseball team he helped manage.[2]

Betting on baseball was commonplace in 1911, regardless of its legality. Partnering with a drifter named George Streplis, a man who had been arrested in March 1911 in Wyoming and held over for trial on gambling charges, Saban had plans to capitalize on the trend of betting on baseball games by urging patrons at saloons in Rawlins to bet heavily

The first picture taken of the Wyoming State Penitentiary All Stars. All the team members are wearing prison-issued shirts with their intake number over the left pocket. The little boy in the center of the All Stars is Warden Alston's son, Felix Alston Jr.   WYOMING STATE ARCHIVES, DEPT. OF STATE PARKS & CULTURAL RESOURCES

on the Death Row All Stars. Any ideas Saban had about placing bets on the penitentiary ball club were tabled, however, until he knew how long Seng would be at the Rawlins facility. He didn't want to gamble on the team if Seng wasn't going to be at the prison long enough to play with the All Stars. An appeal of his sentence had been filed with the governor immediately; on June 15, 1911, Governor Carey responded favorably to the appeal, and on July 18, 1911, the Chief Justice of the state Supreme Court granted a stay of execution in his case.[3]

Regardless of the fact that his time as head of the prison lessee program was coming to an end, Otto Gramm believed he had some lingering influence at the facility. He did own all the equipment and material used to manufacture the brooms, and, as long as that was the case, he would insist on being a part of the business, visiting the penitentiary ostensibly to make sure his property was being maintained properly.[4] He also would be able to monitor other activities at the prison, such as Warden Alston conferring with murderer George Saban on the baseball field. Gramm would have a firsthand look at the players who enjoyed fame of a sort— their names at one time or another resting on the tongues of men who had seen them operate; their faces known, having been posted in newspapers and on sheriffs' boards along with the list of crimes they had committed.

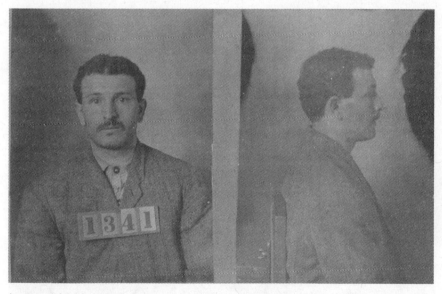

Inmate #1341 Joseph Guzzardo, shortstop. WYOMING STATE ARCHIVES, DEPT. OF STATE PARKS & CULTURAL RESOURCES

Inmate #1459 Eugene Rowan, first baseman. WYOMING STATE ARCHIVES, DEPT. OF STATE PARKS & CULTURAL RESOURCES

Inmate #1477 Sidney Potter, center fielder. WYOMING STATE ARCHIVES, DEPT. OF STATE PARKS & CULTURAL RESOURCES

On July 18, 1911, under a blue and cloudless sky, the murderers, burglars, rapists, and confidence men that made up the Death Row All Stars emerged quickly from the baselines of the baseball diamond at the penitentiary and spread across the practice field for their first game. Alston, Gramm, and a host of other prison officials, as well as inmates, were on hand to watch.[5] Inmates craned their necks to see the action from their barred windows and cheered the players on as they whipped the ball from base to base. Warden Alston had supplied the team with gloves, bats, and uniforms, and the ball club looked and played like professionals. There was no infighting, and players didn't discuss the specifics of their criminal history with one another. The focus was the game.[6]

The stories of the men who took to the field were varied. Shortstop Joseph Guzzardo had killed a woman in 1908 while shooting at a man who was threatening his life. Eugene Rowan, the first baseman, had been convicted of breaking and entering and attempted rape in Cheyenne. Right fielder and catcher James Powell had attacked a young woman. Team captain George Saban had pled guilty to three killings. And catcher and fielder Joseph Seng had been sentenced to death for the murder of a man in Uinta County.[7]

Every time a player came to bat and slapped a ripping fastball on the nose for a solid hit to left field or someone snatched up a red-hot grounder and heaved it to the proper base to get an out, the All Stars forgot they were little more than caged creatures. Warden Alston and Saban stood on the baselines conferring on strategies of the game, discussing when a good bunt would beat a strong hit and how best to utilize each player. But the ever-watchful Gramm believed that their conversation went deeper than that. Prison guard D. O. Johnson had reported to Gramm that Saban was illegally betting on the All Stars' games using money given to him by Warden Alston.[8] Gramm relayed the information to Senator Francis Warren, who suspected the rumor might have a future and that Governor Carey, who had handpicked Warden Alston for the job, was also involved. Senator Warren once said of Governor Carey, "If I hadn't known Carey from the time he stepped off the train in 1869, a green boy up to the present, and hadn't figured inside of the inner circles so much with him in political affairs, he might possibly fool me once in a while, for he surely is the most monumental hypocrite, and the most infernal liar—when necessary— that God ever permitted to live whom I have been permitted to meet."[9]

In spite of the rumors and controversy swirling about, the All Stars won that first official game on July 18, 1911. And the way the team handled their opponent generated a great deal of talk from local business owners and baseball fans about their future. The July 20, 1911, edition of the *Carbon County Journal* called the Death Row All Stars' win over the Wyoming Supply Company Juniors "classy." "Through the kindness of Warden Felix Alston, the Wyoming Supply Company Jrs. went up to the penitentiary Sunday afternoon and played against the Warden's All Star team and was defeated 11 to 1," the article read. "After a short practice game was called and up to the fourth inning neither side could get a run, the Juniors failing to get on first, while the prisoners got to third base in two of the innings. When the prisoners came to bat in the fourth, two men were put out, but they ran in three scores before the third out on errors by the Juniors."

In the next inning they got four men across the plate while the Juniors failed to score. The next inning looked like a shutout again. In the next inning neither side secured a run, although by bunched hits the Juniors got men on all bases.

In the eighth inning the Cons got another home run that brought in two men and the Juniors got their only run, Wallace

Inmate #1480 Earl Stone, one of two alternate pitchers and fielder. WYOMING STATE ARCHIVES, DEPT. OF STATE PARKS & CULTURAL RESOURCES

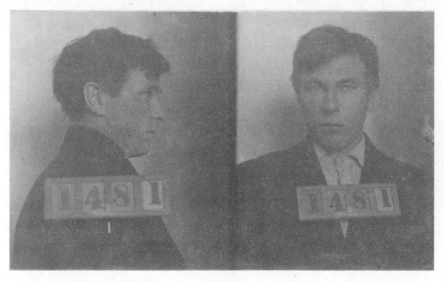

Inmate #1481 Frank Fitzgerald, second baseman. WYOMING STATE ARCHIVES, DEPT. OF STATE PARKS & CULTURAL RESOURCES

making a hit and going to first when Walt Smyth took his place and got around the bags. The ninth was another shutout for the Juniors while the Cons got one more man across home plate.

The prisoners were all out in the yard and yelled and rooted for their team as if they were watching one of the big leagues play.

They made a big barrelful of lemonade and passed it around among the players and spectators alike and put blankets over a clothes rack to make a cool shady place for the Juniors, in fact they did everything to make the visit a most pleasant one and there was no one who realized at the end of the game that they were locked in and playing ball in the stockade of a penitentiary.

Some of the ladies were watching the game from one of the guard houses when one got hit under the eye with a foul ball, the only accident of the game, and many were the expressions of sorrow on the part of the prisoners that this happened.

Joseph Seng, who was convicted of murder in the first degree and sentenced to death, played a classy game all the way through. He will petition the governor to commute his sentence to life imprisonment sometime this month.

Warden Alston has a fast team as our Juniors are classed as one of the best amateur teams in the state and it takes a good team to defeat them, although they were on grounds that were new to them and also that they played one of the oldest games ever played in the state caused them to be a little nervous.

The battery for Sunday's game was: Juniors—Hints and Gunning. Prisoners—Cameron and Powell. The lineup was as follows:

Prisoners	Position	Juniors
Guzzardo	SS	O'Melia
Potter	CF	Bailey

Crottie	*3B*	*Freeman*
Stone	*LF*	*Schalk*
Rowan	*1B*	*Smyth*
Seng	*RF*	*Roberts*
Cameron	*P*	*Hints*
Powell	*C*	*Gunning*
Fitzgerald	*2B*	*Wallace*

The Juniors and visitors wish to thank Warden Alston for the many kindnesses shown at the game and also the prisoners for the delicious lemonade."

Joseph Seng's stellar performance as a hitter and fielder was reported by newspapers from Wyoming to Washington, DC. A headline in the July 24, 1911, edition of the *Washington Post* read SLAYER SCORES HOME RUNS. "A man under death sentence helps convicts win first game," the tagline teased, and the article read, "With a murderer condemned to death as the right fielder, and all other members of the opposing team convicts, the Wyoming Supply Company ball club put up a good game against the Alstons . . ."

While Gramm fought to acquire information to prove his theory that the penitentiary baseball club was Warden Alston's version of the lessee program and that the warden was involved in gambling, Seng fought to survive behind bars. Seng's cell was near that of Lorenzo Paseo, a habitual offender, guilty of a range of crimes from burglary to murder. Paseo was a brash, arrogant man who would battle anyone who defied the authority he thought he had over most inmates. He was not a fan of Warden Alston or of those the warden honored with a spot on the baseball team. According to the book *Annals of Wyoming*, Paseo, along with a few other prisoners in his circle of friends, frequently

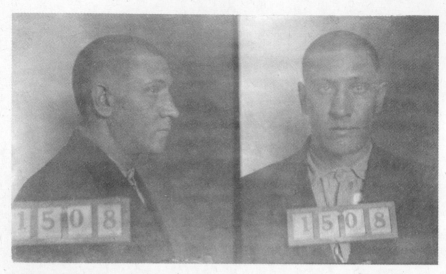

Inmate #1508 Ora Carman, left fielder. WYOMING STATE ARCHIVES, DEPT. OF STATE
PARKS & CULTURAL RESOURCES

Inmate #1532 James Powell, catcher. WYOMING STATE ARCHIVES, DEPT. OF STATE
PARKS & CULTURAL RESOURCES

snuck hair tonic out of the prison barber shop and used it to get drunk. He began most mornings with a drink of the mixture to give him courage to attempt to bully fellow inmates such as Seng. Seng did his best to ignore Paseo and spent a great deal of his free time poring over letters he received from his spiritual advisor in Allentown, Pennsylvania.[10]

Rev. Peter Masson of the Sacred Heart of Jesus Parish in Allentown kept Seng abreast of his family's well-being. Although they had never met, Joseph somehow found it easier to communicate with Masson than with his own brothers, sister, or parents. Some primary sources indicate that Joseph's mother and father knew nothing about their son's situation until March 1912. Joseph was too ashamed to let them know what had happened.[11]

At the urging of Joseph's childhood friends in Pennsylvania, who did finally learn of his dire circumstances, Rev. Masson agreed to have church authorities look into the facts of the case. The result of the church's investigation confirmed that Joseph did act in self-defense in the shooting death of William Lloyd.[12]

Paseo challenged Seng's claim that he had acted in self-defense. He threatened to kill Seng and also continued to make threats against the warden's life. In fact, Paseo's plans for the warden were well known by the general inmate population. Those he could not solicit help from were warned to keep quiet. Seng had no trouble remaining silent on a matter that didn't concern him and went out of his way to avoid men like Paseo. Historical records found in *Annals of Wyoming* note that Seng stayed close to the guards. According to a fellow inmate, "He [Seng] always stood next to the guard's desk when the prisoners were at the dining table. He stood there with his chest thrown out and leaning back against the railing, as though he might be the commander in chief of the army inspecting troops. He would look each convict up and down as he passed by."[13]

Wyoming State Penitentiary historians note that Seng was a helpful prisoner, and, because of that, he was allowed to mingle with other inmates. The majority of inmates were relegated to one area at a time: mess hall, exercise yard, showers, designated cell blocks, etc. The punishment was harsh for anyone who dared defy the rule. Seng's congenial attitude and the ease with which he made his way from one cell block to another without interference from the guards irritated one of Paseo's associates. Seng had favored status, and Paseo's cohorts felt he flaunted his position. Threats were made about killing him, but Seng ignored them.[14]

Warden Alston was coping with similar covert threats issued toward not only himself but also his staff, and rumors of escape plots continued to permeate the facility. Some inmates complained that the warden was unable to establish firm, evenhanded control. Outside the prison, however, the public was gaining confidence in the warden's ability on the job, and he was recognized as a leader with massive political potential. Just prior to the first baseball game the All Stars played, Warden Alston was asked to serve as a delegate to the Wyoming Progress Association Conference in Cheyenne. The Wyoming Progress Association helped organizations develop ideas that would stimulate business in the state.[15]

A newspaper article applauding the work the warden was doing at the prison and how that work was benefitting the community at large was published in the July 14, 1911, edition of the *Big Horn County Rustler*. "Road building by convicts started this morning west of Rawlins when Warden Felix Alston placed a body of prisoners at work," the report read.

This is the beginning of good roads for Wyoming and the redemption in a great measure of convicts. In selecting prisoners for road

Inmate #1569 John Crottie, third baseman. WYOMING STATE ARCHIVES, DEPT. OF STATE PARKS & CULTURAL RESOURCES

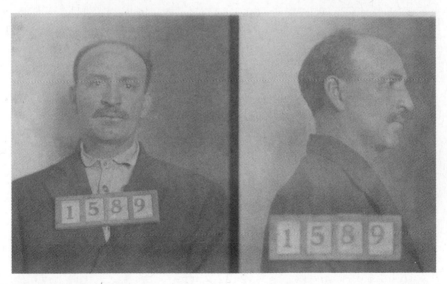

Inmate #1589 H. A. Pendergraft, fielder. WYOMING STATE ARCHIVES, DEPT. OF STATE PARKS & CULTURAL RESOURCES

work, Warden Alston has adopted the policy of men first making good behind the walls before being eligible to work on the roads, and it is needless to say that the prisoners will make every effort to show by their conduct and close application to their work behind the walls that they are worthy of the Warden's confidence and that he can train them to take a place on the road force.

For an overnight of this the first convict gang of road builders, Warden Alston has appointed a man who is serving from twenty to ninety-nine years from Laramie County. The inmate is experienced at this work as well as being very popular with his fellow prisoners and no doubt each man will work his very best for him. You just keep your eyes on Warden Felix Alston and his bunch of road builders for they are going to force you to sit up straight and take some notice.

Warden Alston and L. W. Senville, the man in charge of the broom factory, now under the sole control of the prison and not operated under the lessee agreement, made frequent visits to Cheyenne to update the State Board of Charities and Reform and confer with it on the changes that had been instituted. On August 2, 1911, Warden Alston proudly reported to the board that ten miles of road had been completed since the start of the road-building program. The update he gave on the prison baseball team was even more glowing.[16]

Numerous articles about the baseball team and Joseph Seng in particular appeared in Wyoming newspapers throughout the summer of 1911. Reporters wrote about Seng's ball playing, the team he was a part of, the crime he had been accused of, and whether a judge would commute his sentence from death to life in prison. According to Alta Lloyd's descendants, she considered staying in the area after her husband was shot and killed by Seng. Her family claims she was expecting

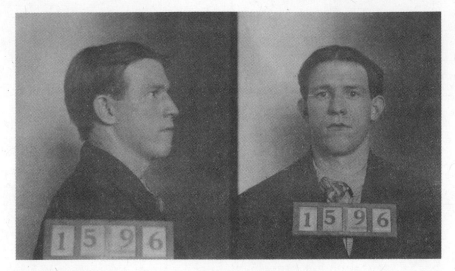

Inmate #1596 Thomas Cameron, pitcher. WYOMING STATE ARCHIVES, DEPT. OF STATE PARKS & CULTURAL RESOURCES

a child and had contemplated living with the Ewers in Evanston while awaiting word about Seng's case.[17] She would have had an opportunity to read the many items printed about him.

Saban's goal was to make 20 percent off the wagers made on the penitentiary team.[18] As captain of the ball club, he had knowledge of the inmate players' strengths and weaknesses, and more important the incentive they had to win. According to Ora Allen, a longtime Wyoming resident and an associate of George Saban, Saban's scheme was well planned. Allen explained to relatives that just prior to the convicts' game with the Juniors on July 18 Saban told oddsmakers that deals had been negotiated between the players and Warden Alston to decrease their prison time and give permanent stays of execution to others if they won all the games the warden had arranged.

Saban persuaded any apprehensive gamblers that he and Warden Alston had significant influence over the All Stars. Given the fact that

Warden Alston had been particularly liberal with Saban's travels to and from the prison and the fact that Saban was captain of the baseball team, gamblers were inclined to believe him.[19] "He let people know that a loss would cost penitentiary players," Allen recalled years later. "I suspect everyone at the top of a plan like that stood to benefit."

The performance of the baseball team members on the field was much more significant to the prison as a whole than the individual accomplishments off the field. All the inmates could share in the glory of a win. The interest in how consistent they were at hitting and fielding was intense, both with fans of baseball and those who wagered on games. Many viewed the prisoners as wanderers from the way who ought to be put back on the right road. If played well, baseball could be their path to righteousness.[20]

CHAPTER SIX

Betting on a Win

Every day Joseph Seng took his usual position beside the guard's desk in the mess hall and studied the inmates as they entered the room. Perhaps this was his way of fighting the monotony and routine of daily prison life. Maybe Seng was trying to assert himself as someone not to be trifled with, or maybe he had no agenda whatsoever. Some convicts believed he was a threat to the position they perceived to hold in the hierarchy of prisoners. Seng didn't worry about what anyone thought of him. He maintained his spot by the desk regardless of the occasional disapproving glance.[1]

In early August 1911 a particularly disagreeable inmate tired of Seng's habit and decided to kill him. The displeased man who wanted Joseph dead wore a ball-and-chain restraint that clanged behind him as he shuffled along. His arms were generally full of the ten-pound ball attached to the iron links. His heavily bearded face was weathered, and his mouth was set in a perpetual snarl that looked inexpressively evil. He gave Seng a rough look as he passed by him and hauled himself and his ball and chain up a flight of steel stairs.[2]

Once the violent inmate made it to the second landing of the facility, he stopped to look out over the people below, his face "filled with rage," according to a story provided by an inmate and included in the *Annals of Wyoming*. "His cell was back at the farthest end of the top gallery," the prisoner recalled. "At the top of the stairs there was a small box of sand about half full for a sort of trash receptacle. The box was about ten inches wide and probably two feet in length. The fellow set the iron ball on the floor of the gallery and picked up a box of sand. He raised it above his head and dropped it straight down at the head of Seng, twenty-five feet almost directly below.

"As the leaden box went down Seng partly turned to speak to the guard and the box struck the floor with a crash like the report of a gun and burst straight through the center sending sand in all directions. If Seng hadn't turned just as he did it would have landed on his head. The fellow picked up the iron ball and went down the gallery to his cell. He had sawed the rivet in two that held the iron on his ankle and as he opened the door he loosened the thing from his leg and threw the ball and chain over the gallery. It struck the table and went straight through the floor leaving a six-foot length of board standing straight up in the center of the table."[3]

Although Seng was shaken by the attempt made on his life, it didn't carry over to his performance on the baseball field. The Death Row All Stars were scheduled to cross bats for a second time with the Wyoming Supply Company Juniors on August 4, 1911. The prison team practiced often in July in preparation for the event.[4]

Even in practices, the Death Row All Stars played with gusto and even temperament. They worked together as one cohesive unit and made the sport look like the easiest game in the world. They seemed to cherish the smell of the leather glove, the snap of the ball smacking their palms, the sensation of letting loose a throw and kicking up a cloud of dust. These were deep pleasures in a world that didn't offer many happy moments, and they relished this one.

Thomas Cameron was in the box for the convicts, throwing one pitch after another in an effort to refuse any hits. Seng was in right field making every catch that came his way. He gobbled up line drives that looked good for a couple of bases at least. At the end of each successful play, the ball would quickly be sent around the bases. James Powell, who was in as catcher, would throw it to Eugene Rowan at first, who would jettison it to Frank Fitzgerald at second. Fitzgerald would whip the ball to John Crottie, who would throw it to Ora Carman in left field. Carman would propel the ball to center fielder Sidney Potter, and Potter would toss it to Seng. Seng, with super-human effort, would send the ball all the way home again.[5]

George Saban watched the roundabout with great interest. He was particularly pleased with the smoke Seng put on the ball. There was an explosive strength in the man's wiry build. Although his teammates offered praise for his effort, Seng looked as if he'd done nothing more thrilling than change a flat tire.

Saban grinned at the talented team as he approached the batter's box. He wanted to hit a few more balls to the players before dusk fell and practice was forced to end. He scraped his spikes into the ground like a bull pawing the earth before he charged. The digits missing on Saban's hands prevented him from gripping the bat as tightly as other players did, but he proceeded as though he had all ten fingers. He scrutinized the pitcher until finally he let the ball fly. Saban connected with the ball. It was a hard grounder that made its way between second and third base. Joseph Guzzardo rushed the ball with his glove poised to scoop it up, but he fumbled the catch. Given how well the team had been doing, the error was glaring. Without missing a beat the pitcher prepared to deliver another throw. George hit another grounder to Guzzardo. Guzzardo fumbled the ball a second time. Frustrated, he marched off the field as though all the try had gone out of him. Saban met him as he headed down the third baseline toward a bench behind home plate.[6]

Seng related the story of what happened next in a letter to Rev. Masson. Saban was furious with Guzzardo over the errors. "He had an expression that let everyone know he had no time for excuses," Seng wrote in late July 1911.[7] "He stomped over to Guzzardo and let him have it. No one could hear what was being said, but something was being said. Guzzardo kept his head down. After a few minutes of serious talk, George motioned for Thomas Cameron to meet him where he stood." Seng's letter went on to explain that Cameron and Guzzardo were both reprimanded—and it wasn't long after the incident that all the players were informed of the particulars of the heated conversation. "Mistakes on the field would not be tolerated," Seng wrote Rev. Masson. "He [Saban] told us that prisoners who make errors that cost the team a game would have more time added to their sentence. Winning would lead to reduced time and stays of execution." Saban told the team those were Warden Alston's terms and that they were non-negotiable. Given Saban's friendship with Warden Alston, no inmate doubted what George said to be true.[8]

To the convict ballplayers, the condition in which they now had to play the game was reminiscent of the lessee program under Otto Gramm. H. A. Pendergraft would later write in the April 25, 1912, edition of the *Laramie Republican*, "That contract labor (in any form) still held the whip-hand at the Wyoming State Penitentiary is in itself good and sufficient evidence that no such reform as claimed had occurred at that institution.

"Beneath its hand and between cogs of its merciless system all the good instincts, all regrets for past misdeeds, all faith in human justice, in human nature, in human sympathy, is crushed and trampled upon," he added. "[It is] a school for crime which flourishes in an age of advanced ideas, where lessons of hate, of discontent and indifference to laws, both human and divine, are instilled into the mind and hearts of men; a market place of shame, an incubator that breeds and nourishes criminal instincts and sends men from prison in a worse state of degradation than when they entered there."

If, as the papers have assured their readers, the prison at Rawlins is being conducted along lines befitting the dignity of a great state and in a manner creditable to the people of Wyoming; If, under the new order of things the prisoners are experiencing great changes for the better in the moral natures and views of life; if their better instincts for right living and proper regard for the common law of society are being developed; if their physical, moral and mental conditions are better than under the old regime; if all this be true, then indeed have the people of Wyoming just cause to be proud of those, who, as their representatives, have brought these admirable results about . . .

You are offered here without prejudice and without malice, to believe or reject according to your own convictions, the real truths, the ground floor facts, "The Other Half of Wyoming State Penitentiary Story," by one who knows and is familiar with existing prison conditions as they actually are.

Prison guard D. O. Johnson and other officials at the prison who were aware of the ultimatum that Saban issued the inmate ball club did not behave as if they felt the idea was out of line. Johnson, who shadowed Saban most everywhere he went, treated the convicts as though they should be grateful for the opportunities they were given, and local gamblers were certainly happy to take advantage of the wagering opportunities that the sport offered above all else.

News of the attempt on Seng's life was a source of much discussion at places like the Klondike Bar. The bookmakers who set up business inside the local saloons and gave the owners of the establishments a portion of their earnings for their troubles were worried about the penitentiary's star player.[9] They wondered whether he would be alive to play the next game and what that meant for the sums that had been wagered on Alston's All Stars to win their next go-round with the Wyoming Supply Company Juniors. Saban was determined to make sure every speculator knew his bets were secure.[10]

Just as it was inside the penitentiary, Saban's reputation and history with Warden Alston carried a great deal of weight with the public at large. George roamed about Carbon County with ease, dressed in civilian clothes and dining with his supporters like a politician campaigning for office. Accompanied by prison guard D. O. Johnson, Saban traveled to the Klondike Bar and the other gaming houses in Rawlins to touch base with those who had funds riding on the baseball club to win. The percentage Saban stood to earn from an All Stars victory promised to be a nice sum, as well. His inside knowledge of the incentive the convict players had been given to win provided him with the confidence he needed to keep gamblers interested and even increase their bets.[11]

Johnson kept Otto Gramm informed about what he knew regarding Saban's gambling ventures. Johnson, who had been hired at the penitentiary by Gramm, felt a sense of loyalty to him. Gramm, of course, liked hearing about problems at the prison and hoped there were more yet to come, so he encouraged Johnson's confidences. Proof of Warden Alston's involvement with Saban's gambling scheme and

Rawlins, Wyoming, on June 9, 1916; the Wyoming State Penitentiary is the tallest building in the center of town. WYOMING STATE ARCHIVES, DEPT. OF STATE PARKS & CULTURAL RESOURCES

Governor Carey's knowledge of the same would go a long way in helping to set things right for Gramm. He was still embittered by Governor Carey's treatment of him and resented how Carey had led the public to believe he was anything less than honest in all his financial dealings. Gramm continued to make Senator Warren aware of the situation. For the moment, however, Senator Warren was content to allow the governor to carry on until the effects of his mismanagement of certain inmates derailed his political career.[12]

When rumors about the open violation of gambling laws reached Governor Carey, he announced to the newspapers his intent to intervene. According to the August 1, 1911, edition of the *Wyoming State Journal*, the governor declared that he would "stop all gambling and illegal liquor sales throughout the state." The *Journal* offered a clue as to why the law had not previously been enforced, reporting that "Local saloon owners say they will obey the order though some claim they were assured last fall of an open season for two years in exchange for their [voting] support."

The All Stars took the field on August 4, 1911, for their second of four games against the Juniors. According to the August 5, 1911, edition of the *Laramie Daily Boomerang*, Seng was the outstanding player of the day. "A game of baseball was played at the penitentiary stockade between the prisoners' team and the Wyoming Supply Company Juniors, in which the prisoners were victorious, winning by a score of 11 to 1," the article read. "Seng, who was convicted at Evanston of murder in the first degree, was one of the star players of the convict team, getting four hits out of four times at bat, and played an errorless game. Seng was sentenced to be hanged on August 29, but will petition the governor to commute his sentence to life imprisonment."

Warden Alston was pleased with the ball club and shared his thoughts about the game with W. H. Veach, the under-sheriff of Big Horn County, who was at the penitentiary the day of the game, delivering a convict to the facility. The lawman told a reporter with the *Sheridan Post* that Warden Alston "seemed to be "making a hit with his new job" and that the "discipline at the state prison was never better." Veach saw not only the baseball team doing well, but the road crews as well. "At present a gang of 40 convicts is at work building roads eight miles from Rawlins," the August 8, 1911, edition of the paper noted. "A lifer acts as night guard, and there is only one civilian with the party and he is the foreman. The workers are practically unguarded, do their own cooking and sometimes they are not seen by the prison authorities from one week's end to another."

Warden Alston's method of prison management was unusual. He seemed to believe that brutal, vengeful punishment only aroused thoughts of violence and blood.[13] Members of the State Board of Charities and Reform, such as state auditor Robert Forsyth, questioned the wisdom of such liberties as allowing prisoners to play ball outside the penitentiary and the use of chain gangs. There was concern from the community and from officials who opposed Alston's reforms that the public might be at risk from certain dangerous criminals.

Alston's practices and attitudes were right in line with research of the day. According to studies done in 1911 on the outdoor treatment of crime by Harris R. Cooley, a minister and prison reform leader, the traditional feeling that severe and painful punishment exterminates wrong thoughts and acts was medieval. "Under the old system," Harris wrote in February 1911, "the hope of the prisoner was to conceal and utterly deny all wrong-doing. This very act closed for him personally the doorway to better living. . . . We are expending for the detection and punishment of crime nearly twice as much as for education, charity, and religion combined.

Harris continued, "A general change of attitude toward the so-called 'criminal classes' is the fundamental thing which is happening. Prophetic minds have heralded the new spirit of human fellowship, and here and there individuals have had faith to try the discipline of kindness. All are now coming to see the possibility and wisdom of preventing and curing crime. . . . In a number of institutions the outdoor methods have been tried with marked success. Few violate the trust given them, whether it's working in fields, on railroads, building roads, or recreational sporting programs."[14]

According to Alston's grandson Scott Alston, the warden was "sincere in trying to improve the conditions at the prison" and toward that end instituted a lot of reforms.[15] The baseball team was one of many such endeavors. Still, Gramm never ceased being suspicious of the warden's motives, and Saban helped fan the flame of mistrust through his activities outside the prison walls. In the days after the All Stars' win, Johnson escorted Saban to the local taverns to brag about the team and collect on his wagers and likely reported back to Gramm about Saban's actions.[16]

Gramm's animosity toward Governor Carey and Warden Alston had been growing. The grudge was solidified when the governor insisted Gramm be removed from the Board of Trustees at the University of Wyoming in Laramie.[17] Then, for the second time since he had been in office, Governor Carey publicly implied that Gramm had misappropriated funds. An article in the June 23, 1911, edition of the *Laramie Republican* suggested that the governor was wrong to remove Gramm from the board and that some University of Wyoming board members believed Governor Carey needed to admit his error. The piece read in part, "No well-informed voter believed for a minute there was anything wrong going on at the university. It was only those who were not advised to conditions and who were willing to take the word of such men as Governor Carey. The *Republican* is advised that even the Governor has stated on the quiet to members of the university board that he was misinformed about some matters, and that he now approves all that the board did in the disposition of the university hands. He simply lacks the courage to come before the people and frankly state that he deceived them and the great crime by which the people are robbed of $500,000 was a myth conjured up in a brain anxious to get hold of the reins of government—with little care to the methods."

Gramm's reputation had suffered because of Governor Carey's allegations of malfeasance, and he was becoming more determined to bring about the governor's, as well as Warden Alston's, downfall. Johnson, however, had proved unwilling to give any specifics about who was betting on the All Stars and how much money was changing hands. Governor Carey had previously countered rumors of gambling by issuing a statement noting that "all officials are charged to enforce the anti-gaming laws without fear or favor."[18] Bookmakers were indifferent to the admonition and admitted to reporters at the *Wyoming State Journal* that "the crop of tame suckers was very short this year."[19] Trouble at the penitentiary involving convicts who were threatening to escape and Lorenzo Paseo and his cohorts railing against Joseph Seng offered Gramm a modest amount of consolation.[20]

In spite of the promise offered by the reforms he had instituted, Warden Alston was so overwhelmed with tackling the difficulties inside the penitentiary that he didn't have much time to revel in his baseball team's wins against the Juniors. An inmate at the state prison admitted in writing that there was a plot to assassinate the warden in the summer of 1911.[21] The warden was able to isolate the instigators of the plan and had them placed in a separate lockup from the rest of the general population.[22]

The warden made sure the guards accounted for every inmate every day at roll call. Those who did not appear and were suspected of hiding somewhere in the prison were subject to punishment. Diminutive prisoners known as "human ferrets" were often sent to locate inmates hiding on the grounds. According to the *Annals of Wyoming*, a "human ferret was a short, small prisoner who was used to search under buildings and through heating tunnels for the miscreant."[23]

Warden Alston hoped the strict rule for roll call attendance would persuade Seng's enemies to keep their distance from his star player.

He was also genuinely working on bettering general conditions and hoped the installation of screens on the windows throughout the prison and improvements to the restroom would ease the tension between the inmates and administration. His efforts didn't pay off.[24] A pair of inmates escaped custody and broke out of the prison on August 9, 1911. According to the August 10, 1911, edition of the *Rawlins Republican,* "Two prisoners, Frank Frunirp and W. L. Peterson, who were employed at the road camp west of the city, got tired of their jobs and on Thursday night of last week started out to look for something different." The article went on: "Warden Felix Alston was notified at once and a wire was sent out along the rail line to locate the escapees. The Union Pacific Railroad police located them on Monday and notified Sheriff McCourt of Green River and the officer followed them to the hills about twenty miles north of the Green River and captured them.

"Sheriff McCourt and Warden Alston returned with the prisoners on Tuesday evening. Both men only had a few more months to serve and one of them would have been released in October. They will both lose the good time that was in the credit and it is not probable that they will get their old position on the road gang."

In the meantime the public was clamoring for a chance to see Alston's "fast team" take the field. On August 4, 1911, the *Carbon County Journal* announced that the Death Row All Stars might play outside the prison walls. "Warden Alston of the penitentiary has informed us that to comply with a general demand to see his fast team of convict ball players play he has a plan in mind wherein he can take the team down to the fairgrounds for a game with the Wyoming Supply Company Jrs. team," the article began.

The warden asks that all who attend this game go to the grandstand and not to go out on the diamond while the teams are playing, and

*all who attend will observe this rule or it may be the only oppor-
tunity of ever seeing the team play ball. Another game will be held
in the penitentiary yard in the near future for the benefit of the
prisoners, before the downtown game, but the public is excluded
from this one.*

*The prisoners have developed some strong teamwork and will
put up a first class game with any team in the state. In a game
played at the Pen a short time ago they defeated the Juniors 11 to
1, and everyone knows the Juniors are playing a good article of
ball, but they attribute their defeat to nervousness and think they
can defeat the convicts in the other games to be played. Be on the
lookout for the date of the downtown game and take it in; you will
be assured to see one of the best games of the season.*

The Wyoming Supply Company team was organized by Daniel
C. Kinnaman, the owner of the company and a trustee of the city of
Rawlins. The building plumbing and supply business was one of the
most respected companies in Carbon County. It provided services to
the penitentiary, specifically to the broom factory. The team was made
up of young men in their late teens and early twenties. They were an
exceptional ball club and were considered one of the best bush league
teams in the country. Kinnaman proposed a handful of games with
Alston's All Stars to help them with their training and improve their
abilities. Until the Juniors experienced their first loss at the hands of
the penitentiary team, friendly wagers were placed on them to beat the
All Stars at every meeting.[25]

Even in the midst of success on the field, problems were rife at
the penitentiary. Another setback for Warden Alston's administration
occurred on August 15, 1911, when guard W. F. Carrick was shot and
killed by an unknown assailant.[26] "Carrick had turned in his clock, as

is the watchman's duty every hour, and had returned to the rear of the building to look around and saw that the other guards in the office and cell house were on duty," an article in the August 17, 1911, edition of the *Rawlins Republican* read. "He then returned to the office . . . and was returning to the rear of the building again and just as he opened the gate he was shot in the head with a bullet from a Winchester. It is thought that someone on the outside had gone to the penitentiary with the intentions of liberating a friend. A rope ladder and several steel hacksaws were found on the prison fence. Carrick had just recently come from Texas and had only worked at the penitentiary three nights."

The convicts' attempted escape and the death of the guard worried Rawlins's citizens and called into question the wisdom of allowing inmates to be involved in any activities outside the prison walls. Games the Death Row All Stars were scheduled to play were now in jeopardy of being cancelled. The future of the team was in limbo.[27]

CHAPTER SEVEN

Nothing but the Game

Photographer M. F. Jukes squeezed the rubber bulb attached to the camera standing next to him, and a bright white flash lit up a section of the penitentiary dining hall. When the flash faded Alston's All Stars became visible. Dressed in dark uniforms and corresponding caps with the initials WSP stitched across the front and carrying well-worn baseball gloves, team members held their proud pose until Jukes gave them permission to relax. The men talked among themselves as the prominent Rawlins photographer adjusted the shutters around the lens in preparation for the next shot. A sign among his camera equipment on a nearby table read, "Pictures in black and white or Sepia finish, on stiff cards, folders or flexible mountings. Various prices, one of which will suit your pocket. Come in at any time, or if more desirable, phone for an appointment. Settings done upon request. Most locations acceptable."[1]

At the appropriate time each player resumed his position for another picture to be taken. The first time the prisoners had gathered together for a photograph, they had been dressed in the clothing issued to them by the penitentiary officials as part of their incarceration. The inmate numbers they had been assigned were scrawled over the left breast pocket of their shirts, and the baseball equipment they held consisted of castoffs from players who had abandoned the game some time ago. In this photo, taken after their first wins, the convicts were different in dress and style. Their coordinating outfits gave them an air of professionalism. Some reverently cradled in their arms the gloves and baseballs they would use in upcoming games; others wore their mitts on their hands to show how ready they were to play.[2]

Joseph Seng stood on the left end of the back row with his hand on his hip. His mustache was neatly trimmed, and his cap was pulled down low on his forehead. His serious expression conveyed that he was a fierce opponent to other teams. Convicted rapist Eugene Rowan stood on Seng's right, and beside him was George Saban. Saban's shoulders were pulled back as though he were at attention. The top button of his shirt was undone, his neck being too thick to allow him to fasten it. Swindler Earl Stone, gambler and attempted rapist James Powell, and larcenist H. A. Pendergraft were on Saban's right. Four-year-old Felix Vern Alston Jr. sat on a stool just below Saban wearing a dark blue uniform, stockings, and dark blue cap. On either side of him were murderer Joseph Guzzardo and thief Frank Fitzgerald; condemned rapist Thomas Cameron and burglar John Crottie bookended the bottom row.[3]

The photograph was proudly displayed in the warden's office. Felix Jr., whom Alston had made the team mascot, is in the middle of the criminal offenders, wearing the team's uniform and smiling at the camera. Nothing in the team photo would have led anyone to imagine that the players had run afoul of the law.

In mid-August 1911 Saban was still a frequent guest at the Klondike Bar, which was attracting business due to the straight betting on

Warden Alston's son poses with members of the Wyoming State Penitentiary All Stars. Joseph Seng is in the back row, far left. WYOMING STATE ARCHIVES, DEPT. OF STATE PARKS & CULTURAL RESOURCES

the convict baseball game that patrons could indulge in there. According to historian Rans Baker, the establishment enjoyed a fair amount of activity, but it was rarely crowded. It was a favorite stop for miners, railroad employees, and local businessmen, and Saban and guard D. O. Johnson were always treated courteously there. According to historian Duane Shillinger, the Klondike Bar wasn't doing anything other taverns weren't doing. Under-the-table gambling was an expected accompaniment to the Old Pepper Whisky and Old McBrayer Bourbon they served. "At the time," Shillinger noted, "every baseball game played in Rawlins, prisoner or otherwise, was bet on at the gambling dens."[4]

Among the characters that kept company with Saban at the different saloons in town was Ora Allen. Allen held a variety of jobs in Wyoming and Colorado. He was a prospector with a copper claim and had invested heavily in a mining development company; he was a farmer with a family ranch that he worked with his brother; he was a land speculator, he was a father, and he was a gambler. Allen also owned and operated a hack line, a stable of horses used for trail rides. The business was called Huskin and Allen, and he not only used the horses to take groups out in a long line trail ride, but also employed the animals when he traveled to his out-of-the-way mining claims.[5] He also may have used the horse business as a cover for the money he collected for Saban. He reasoned that suspicious authorities would be less likely to catch him on horseback as he rode into the mountains to his claims.[6]

Allen and Saban made a good team.[7] Allen carried Saban's message about Warden Alston's influence over the team's players to saloons in Cheyenne and Thermopolis, repeating Saban's assertions that the warden had promised to lessen the inmate ballplayers' prison time and stay executions if the team continued winning. When necessary to drive up the number of wagers, Allen also relayed the threat to death row inmates about ending their lives if they lost a game.[8]

On August 13, 1911, the Wyoming State Penitentiary All Stars were dutifully led onto the baseball field at the prison by a handful of guards. The Wyoming Supply Company Juniors were waiting for them, and the spectators in attendance erupted in applause for the teams and cheered in anticipation of the game about to be played. The August 17, 1911, edition of the *Rawlins Republican* included a succinct article about the game entitled "Prisoners Win Again." It began, "Another game of baseball was played Sunday morning at the penitentiary between Warden Alston's All Stars and the Wyoming Supply Company Jrs. Rich Magor was in the box for the Juniors and pitched a fine game considering that his arm was hurt in the game against Junction City. Thomas Cameron was in the box for the pen boys and plainly showed that he was 'there and over' in the pitcher's class."

The outcome of the matchup was covered in more detail by the August 18, 1911, edition of the *Carbon County Journal*. Entitled "Ball at Pen," the column explained how the Juniors were "outclassed."

The Juniors were the first up to bat and Brady, the Juniors' third baseman, fanned out. The Juniors could not get a hit and failed to reach first. Magor, the Juniors' pitcher, let the first convict walk, but he was thrown out at second. They got men on second and third but were retired before they made a run.

The Juniors did better in the second getting one run home. Joseph Seng was put out going to first, and then Frank Fitzgerald knocked a three base hit that scored a run. The next inning was a shutout for the Juniors, Magor getting as far as third base before the side was retired. The same thing happened to the convicts, no runs being made on either side in this inning.

Wallace of the Juniors made a run after two men were out in the fourth inning and the convicts got two runs. O'Melia, the Juniors' shortstop, made the star hit for the Juniors, getting a home run in the fifth inning, but the bases were empty and the best he could do was to tie the score. The convicts didn't want it tied and put two men over the home plate before they were retired.

The sixth inning was another shutout for the Juniors while the cons got one more man across the plate. Magor's arm seemed to go to pieces and the convicts all hit the ball for a base or two.

The seventh was another one-two-three-you're out inning for the Juniors while the cons got in three scores. One run was made by the Juniors in the eighth and they played hard to get another run, but were retired before they could get another man home and the convicts got two more runs before their side was out.

The ninth inning was a big zero for both sides and the game ended by the score of 11 to 4 in favor of the convicts. The following is the box score of the game.

Convicts

	AB	R	H	PO	A	E
Guzzardo, SS	4	0	1	1	2	1
Potter, CF	5	1	2	0	0	1
Crottie, 3B	5	1	1	2	0	0
Carman, LF	5	1	3	0	0	1
Rowan, 1B	5	2	2	4	1	0
Seng, RF	5	2	2	0	0	0
Powell, C	4	2	2	15	4	0
Fitzgerald, 2B	4	2	3	5	1	0
Cameron, P	4	0	1	0	2	0
Totals	36	11	17	27	10	3

Juniors

	AB	R	H	PO	A	E
Brady, 3B	4	1	1	1	0	0
Smith, 1B	4	0	0	6	1	1
Bailey, CF	3	0	0	0	2	0
Schalk, LF	2	1	0	0	0	0
Wallace, 2B	3	1	1	3	0	0
Daley, RF	3	0	0	0	0	0
Gunning, C	4	0	0	13	2	1
O'Melia, SS	3	1	2	1	1	3
Magor, P	3	0	2	0	3	0
Totals	29	4	6	24	9	5

Otto Gramm was traveling from Laramie and Cheyenne back to Rawlins when the Death Row All Stars played their third official game against the Juniors. Gramm was on the board of directors for the Laramie-Hahns Peak Railroad and needed to attend to business. High-grade iron ore had been found on Muddy Mountain that interfered with the laying of the railroad track.[9] Gramm was preoccupied not only with the idea that the line would need to be rerouted, but also with trying to capitalize on the rich find. Gold was instantly found at the location, and Gramm was anxious to determine whether more of the substance might still be there along with the iron ore. He learned of the All Star win through the *Rawlins Republican* newspaper.[10] Given the popularity of the team and comments made by Warden Alston in the August 4, 1911, edition of the *Carbon County Journal* about the "general demand to see his fast team play," Gramm anticipated that more games would be scheduled.

Gramm's wife had plans for him to escort her to their sheep ranch outside Laramie for an extended stay. The couple would not return to Rawlins until August 20, and at that time Gramm intended to meet with prison guard D. O. Johnson and Warden Alston. Gramm was convinced that prison officials were benefitting monetarily from the inmate baseball team. Just as Governor Carey insisted the public be made aware of the "true records" of Gramm's prison management and emoluments, and "who, if any were his partners," Gramm demanded the same of Warden Alston's administration.

During the summer of 1911, as the All Stars were proving their mettle on the field, Governor Carey was spending a great deal of time on issues relating to the state prison and the convicts housed there. In addition to dealing with critics who believed Felix Alston was the wrong man for the job of warden, Carey recommended the pardon of fifteen prisoners, including a woman named Annie Bruce, and he responded to a letter pleading for the life of Joseph Seng.[11] Anna Seng, Joseph's forty-nine-year-old mother, had written Governor Carey to try to spare her son from being put to death.[12]

"Esteemed and Dear Sir," Anna's letter began.

> *Your Honor will graciously allow the almost despairing mother of Joseph Seng now preparing for death, in jail at Rawlins, to intercede most humbly for his pardon. I was always hoping that a new trial might at least change the awful sentence. I do not want to criticize justice done in the case. Only I beg Your Honor to spare the life of my son, who had certainly received a good education at home.*
>
> *I cannot express in words what I have suffered since I got the awful news, not being able to lend, my dear son, any financial aid in his trial. I am afraid even to tell my hard working husband anything of this case, as the sad news might kill him and deprive the large family of its only support.*
>
> *I shall ever be grateful to you for any act of benign clemency. I am sure also that my unfortunate son will prove himself deeply grateful for such an act and turn a new leaf.*
>
> *Hoping and praying that my humble prayer will meet with your mind's acceptance. I remain, Mrs. Anthony Seng. Yours gratefully forever.[13]*

After careful consideration Governor Carey penned an answer to the desperate mother.

"Dear Madam, I have your letter of the 9th instant. Before I received your letter I had acquainted myself somewhat with the facts in the trial and conviction of Joseph Seng. You are his mother, and I have no doubt you are greatly distressed. He murdered his victim and gave him no chance whatever for his life. I will look into the matter further, but, to be entirely honest with you, at this time I do not see any excuse whatever for execution clemency in his case."[14]

Joseph's spiritual advisor and confidant, Rev. Peter Masson from the Sacred Heart of Jesus Parish in Allentown, Pennsylvania, also wrote Governor Carey about the condemned man. "Esteemed and kind Sir," the letter began. "Kindly allow me to intercede for an almost despairing mother. She has a son, Joseph Seng, in jail in Rawlins. If it should be possible to commute his sentence, I most humbly ask you to have pity on the poor mother and her large family. Very respectfully and gratefully, Peter Masson."[15]

Governor Carey's response, dated July 15, 1911, was thoughtful and to the point. "Dear Sir, I have your letter making an appeal for Joseph Seng. I have given this matter some consideration and find there are not extenuating circumstances in this case. In cold blood he took the life of his victim and did not ever give him a chance to defend himself. I am sorry for his people, but he who breaks the law must suffer the penalty. Very truly yours, Governor J. Carey."

Life at the penitentiary for Seng was more than just waiting for the next baseball game. At an early age he'd worked in a drugstore, helping the pharmacist shelve medicine and keep inventory, and in prison he discovered that he had an aptitude for medicine.[16] According to Dr. Griffith Maghee, who was the newly appointed surgeon for the state prison, Seng could "perceive relationships and connections among symptoms and a patient to determine his condition." Maghee was so impressed with Seng's skill that he made him his assistant. Seng's job entailed helping to take a patient's vital signs and administering basic first aid. The ten-bed medical unit at the prison contained only the most rudimentary medicine, bandages, and splints. Inmates suffering from serious illnesses were sent to a hospital off-site. A massive glass window at one end of the dispensary faced the gallows. The grim view no doubt helped injured or sick patients on to a speedy recovery. Dr. Maghee recognized potential in Seng and encouraged his natural aptitude in medicine. He gave Seng the opportunity to learn all he could about working in a dispensary. Outside the rudimentary task of maintaining the inventory of the bandages, headache tablets, and other basic healthcare supplies, Seng also helped monitor inmates who needed regular care. Regardless of his interest in the field, and the many hours spent working with the prison physician, nothing stood in the way of baseball practice.[17]

By the end of the summer in 1911, many penitentiary inmates suspected that Seng had lost any legal appeal to sustain his life. Many prisoners also believed that the only thing standing in the way of the immediate execution of the star ballplayer was his success on the baseball field. The brutal Lorenzo Paseo, who was originally scheduled to be hanged in August 1910 for the murder of a man named Charles Cole, had received a commutation of sentence to life in prison and was fighting for a complete dismissal of the conviction based on his idea that he did not get a fair trial and that the evidence was insufficient. Paseo resented being treated like a criminal by prison officials.[18] And he resented Joseph Seng.

One of the many reasons Paseo disliked Seng so much was the fact that Seng enjoyed a certain respect from the guards and prison employees like Dr. Maghee. Paseo's resentment of other prisoners often manifested itself in violence. He had spent time in solitary for challenging W. H. "Cap" Brine, the chief cell house guard, and for stabbing a fellow inmate. In the summer of 1911, Dr. Maghee and his inmate assistant had helped tend to the seriously injured victim's deep wounds before he was hurried away to the hospital at Rock Springs.[19] Seng's presence at the scene further enraged Paseo, whom most inmates referred to as a madman. As he was being hauled away to the dungeon, Paseo issued a warning to Seng "to watch himself" or he'd make sure Seng "never played another baseball game again."[20] According to the February 13, 1912, edition of the *Laramie Republican*, the "feeling among the prisoners against Lorenzo Paseo was very strong, and officials feared that if Paseo was released from solitary the inmates would kill him." [21]

Paseo was also behind an escape plot at the prison. "The Mexican proposed that we make a break . . ." one of the Wyoming State Penitentiary inmates recalled in a biennial report compiled by the State Board of Charities and Reform in 1911. "He proposed that we arm ourselves with knives," the inmate continued, "and when the Warden came around we would capture him and threaten to inflict diverse forms of butchery upon his person with wicked looking broom knives." The plan was thwarted by an experienced guard.[22]

Not all of the guards were as dedicated to maintaining order at the prison. Several of the guards employed there had been incarcerated at one time and had once worked for Otto Gramm, yet Warden Alston had kept them on, much to the dismay of the prisoners. Dissatisfied convicts decided to make plans to escape the prison and the dishonest guards. In addition, Paseo went to great extremes to try to discredit Seng with the warden and the team.[23] Determined to take advantage of the disharmony among the warden, guards, and inmates, Paseo saw his chance to make more trouble for Seng one evening when a prisoner named Black tried to break out.[24]

Black was discovered missing one night after dinner in late August 1911. Guards were sent to look for him and to pressure other inmates about what they might know of his disappearance. Black, who had been recovering from a head injury, was last seen in his cell. When guards searched the cell, all that was found were blankets on the bunk shaped to look like a body lying under them. A loaf of bread with bandages tied around it was used for the head. Paseo accused Seng of stealing the bread and giving it to Black. Seng vehemently denied the claim.[25]

A thorough search of the facility was ordered and a prisoner known as Lindsey was called in to help. Lindsey was one of the penitentiary's human ferrets. After two days Lindsey found Black. The man had been hiding in the combustion chamber of one of the boilers.[26]

As the summer wore on, Seng made a point to avoid Paseo and those inmates under his influence. He concentrated on preparing for the next baseball game (scheduled for August 27, 1911), his work with Dr. Maghee, and his hoped-for stay of execution. More than four months had passed since a jury had heard evidence against him in the slaying death of William Lloyd.

Seng's scheduled execution date, August 22, 1911, had come and gone, and he remained alive to consider the events that had led to his incarceration and to wonder how he could prolong his life. Fellow teammates such as H. A. Pendergraft felt the conditions at the prison were so bad that inmates would rather die than go on. "There is no night school at the penitentiary, no school of any kind apart from the school conducted by the Laramie Broom Company," he wrote in an open letter that would appear in the April 25, 1912, edition of the *Laramie Republican*.

The same mode of punishment for the infraction of the prison rules is in vogue as under the old administration. Prisoners are without sufficient oil in their lamps to last during the hours in which they are confined to their cells, and, consequently, are compelled to lose what short time is theirs by right to read or instruct themselves in other ways. It has been claimed that the heating plant has been practically renewed. Perhaps it has. If one new stack and a few minor pipe fittings constitute the renewing of a heating plant, then, certainly, the heating plant of the Wyoming state prison has been renewed.

As to the hours of labor at the prison, they have been increased, also a greater demand for production from shop operators is required than was formerly under the old administration. Several prisoners work on Sundays as well as week days. They are not compelled to do so, of course, but a good prison record is not to be jeopardized, and as a matter of policy these men forfeit their Sunday and holiday nights to the call of the system.

To be placed on a broom machine is in many cases regarded as a form of punishment, for it is very well understood among the prisoners who operate broom tying machines that their chances of being released on parole or in any other manner until the expiration of their time, are reduced to the minimum.

When Seng stepped onto the ball field and took his position around the diamond, nothing in the way he played led spectators to think his mind was on anything other than the game. George Saban worked the team hard during their practice session at the penitentiary before the next game as Warden Alston and a clutch of guards stood near the home plate backstop watching the activity.

After the August 15 murder of the prison guard W. F. Carrick, less than two weeks before the Death Row All Stars were to meet the Wyoming Supply Company Juniors again, security was at a heightened state. The extra scrutiny resulted in a few fumbles by the players, but it was nothing they couldn't overcome with a powerful throw or fast running. Occasionally the warden would call Saban over to him to discuss something. Saban would return to his post each time and dispatch the ball harder and bark at the team to try harder—nothing less would be tolerated.[27]

On August 21, 1911, Gramm returned to Rawlins after a brief stay at his sheep ranch outside of Laramie, and prison guard D. O. Johnson finally gave Gramm an estimate of how much money had changed hands as a result of the All Stars' latest win. He reiterated what George Saban had told him regarding Warden Alston's part in the betting and wagering on the All Stars. Gramm's antagonism and resentment was further inflamed by the news.[28]

Gramm continued to suspect that the improprieties extended to the governor's office. He again reached out to Senator Warren, who needed Gramm's support for his reelection campaign. Gramm's goals were to have Senator Warren end the tenures of both Warden Alston and Governor Carey—and to end the careers of the members of Alston's All Stars. He hoped the outcome of Senator Warren's actions would result in his position at the prison being fully restored by the winter of 1911.[29]

The last game the Death Row All Stars played against the Wyoming Supply Company Juniors was held on August 27, 1911. The citizenry of Rawlins and surrounding towns poured into Overland Park and found a seat in the stands to watch the matchup. Lovers of the national pastime were not disappointed with the meeting. The Juniors had a reputation for being an efficient ball club. They had played several games with opponents from Rock Springs and Laramie and had arrived on the other side victorious. They had not been so lucky when coming up against the penitentiary team. Wyoming Supply Company owner (and Juniors sponsor) Daniel C. Kinnaman had begun his association with the state prison in the early 1900s. The building supplier provided the institution with material needed for various construction jobs. When Warden Alston assembled his baseball squad, Kinnaman couldn't resist accepting a challenge that his team compete against the inmates.[30]

Apart from the three losses Alston's All Stars had handed the Juniors, Kinnaman's boys had lost only one other game since they began playing in May 1911. In mid-July 1911 the Laramie Juniors beat the Rawlins-based team 9 to 5. According to the July 28, 1911, edition of the *Carbon County Journal* "costly errors on the part of the Wyoming Supply Company Jrs. is what cost the game, allowing the Laramie men to score on most of their errors." The article mentioned that the game wasn't very well attended and that "the boys failed to get money enough to pay the team's extra expenses." "They are a classy bunch of ball players and deserve your support," the report concluded.

On August 31, 1911, the *Rawlins Republican* newspaper noted that the good-size crowd that had turned out to watch the Juniors and the Death Row All Stars was excited and "there was much enthusiastic rooting for both sides." The article doesn't elaborate on what specific player was the most valuable All Star; it merely mentions that "there are a few classy players among the prisoners and that they all under-stand the game." "The Juniors did not play up to their usual standard," the report continues, "and in consequence the prisoners captured the game by the score of 15 to 10."

After their win against the Juniors, the Death Row All Stars were escorted back to prison to await notification of the next practice or game. The inmates surrendered their gloves, bats, balls, and uniforms, and since no matches were pending, they were left to only imagine time on the baseball field. Talk at the penitentiary centered on the possibility of prisoners attending school and not playing baseball. The warden was considering a plan to have the educated convicts teach inmates who had never had the advantage of school. Local politicians thought a school in the prison would be of great benefit to the inmates and society at large. Dr. Maghee committed to teach the basic fundamentals of medicine and hoped that Seng would take advantage of the class should the idea be approved by the Wyoming State Board of Charities and Reform.[31]

Seng couldn't see himself doing anything but perfecting his game and trying to stay alive. Not only was there the question of his execution being scheduled, but also there were continued problems with a portion of the prison population that threatened his well-being. Lorenzo Paseo and his followers had never wavered from their desire to want to harm members of the warden's baseball club, especially Seng.

CHAPTER EIGHT

Dead Man at Bat

In November 1911 winter weather had moved in, and the Wyoming State Penitentiary infirmary was filled to near overflowing with violently ill inmates. Patients with no beds to lie on sat on the floor, propped up against the wall. Some were drawn into a fetal position and others were draped facedown across thin pillows scattered around the room. The air was pungent and oven-hot. The sound of sick convicts retching into buckets and tin pans echoed throughout the crowded medical unit.[1]

Joseph Seng hurried from one patient to another, assisting Dr. Maghee. He mopped the damp sweat off the prisoners' heads, gave them drinks of water, and fed them chips of ice. Guards escorted more ailing men into the medical unit and dropped them wherever they could find space. The sick inmates moaned in pain and some cried out for relief.[2]

After several hours of listening to the suffering, collecting the vital signs of each patient, and analyzing the symptoms, the doctor and his assistant determined that the men, including several members of the baseball team, had been poisoned. News of their illness and speculation that the poisoning might have been a deliberate act spread quickly throughout the prison. Several prison guards, including D. O. Johnson, considered the possibility that someone with a grudge against the penitentiary baseball team and its chance to compete in future games might have orchestrated the poisoning.[3] There was some chatter between the guards and prisoners that Otto Gramm could be behind the trouble.[4]

Gramm, naturally, was not unhappy about the news that problems were still plaguing the prison under Warden Alston's watch. He was rumored to have been offended by a column that had appeared in the November 3, 1911, edition of the Lander, Wyoming, newspaper the *Lander Eagle*. The headline read Carey Saving Good Money— Better Than Gramm. The article that followed contained a statement of the affairs of the Wyoming State Penitentiary and showed significant improvements on financial and other fronts. "The people are entitled to know and the books of the administration are open to all," Governor Carey was quoted in the report. "The results of the administration of the penitentiary under the new arrangement can best be summed up by presenting a statement of what the penitentiary [would have] cost the state had Otto Gramm been allowed to remain in his position there," the article continued.

"It's shown that the average daily per capita cost to the state was $.61 cents for the year ending September 30, 1910, made up by the $.50 cents per day per prisoner paid to Mr. Otto Gramm, lessee, and the $.11 cents per day per prisoner paid for permanent improvements, discharge money, etc. Had the Gramm contract continued the expense to that would have been more than $25,000.00."

Luckily, with Seng's help, Dr. Maghee was able to relieve the prisoners of their misery. The pair mixed a concoction of mustard and

Coca-Cola that helped to purge the toxins from the sick convicts. Patients and prison officials praised the doctor and Seng for bringing an end to the outbreak. Within twenty-four hours of the incident occurring, health had been restored and inmates returned to their cells.[5] According to the November 6, 1911, edition of the *Laramie Daily Boomerang,* the cause of the poisoning turned out to be contaminated food. "A quantity of kraut had been allowed to remain in a metal pot overnight," the article read, "and along the edge had absorbed poison and in a few minutes after eating it many prisoners were in intense pain."

George Saban kept himself clear of any disputes with fellow inmates and aligned himself with more than one guard who had an allegiance to Otto Gramm. Saban had a problem with other prisoners only when they stood in the way of his money-making ventures. News that law enforcement was cracking down on illegal gambling throughout the state was the basis for his frustration that fall, beginning in September 1911.[6]

Saban had become aware of a novel method of betting on baseball results after reading a regional newspaper and was looking forward to putting it into practice in Rawlins. Those who wanted to place a wager on a game need not root for any special club or league or be interested in the outcome of a particular match. According to the September 22, 1911, edition of the *Cheyenne State Leader*, all gamblers needed to know was how many runs would be made by a specific player or by the team as a whole. The game, which was being run above a saloon in Chicago, attracted more than eight thousand participants in one week. The minimum bet was fifty cents. "The ticket having the name of the team combination which makes the most runs in the week is the winner of the first prize," the article explained. Promoters took 10 percent of the pool for their services. "Patrons were flocking to the saloon," the report continued, "to watch the score to see how their chances were running."[7]

As much as Saban wanted to try his luck with the system, he felt as though he needed to rein in his unlawful activities until the focus of the police shifted away from gaming. His instincts proved to be right. Near the northern border of the state, law enforcement made a number of arrests in Cody in a single night's gambling raid. According to the November 22, 1911, edition of the Cody daily newspaper the *Park County Enterprise*, proof that gambling was indeed going on came when authorities raided a saloon called Chapman's. Patrons playing "twenty-one" for drinks were arrested, as was the owner of the establishment. Friends of the saloonkeeper told the *Enterprise* reporter that he had been made the victim of "discrimination and persecution." "They insisted that the little game was stopped by the officers the same night there were two big games going on behind locked doors, but these were not molested," the article read.

The news on the street was that Governor Carey had ordered the raid and would order more in an effort to put a stop to gambling everywhere in Wyoming. Opponents of the governor said he was "selective" about what establishments he decided to raid and challenged him to look within his own sphere of influence if he was sincere about doing away with gambling.[8]

According to Warden Alston's grandson, Scott Alston, Governor Carey sent a letter to the prison in early September 1911 expressing his concern about the baseball team. Some citizens were not only critical of the fact that the All Stars were allowed to play ball outside the stockades of the prison but were also opposed to the idea that state officials might be wagering on the team. "This must not be done," the governor warned regarding the baseball club playing further games outside the penitentiary. "Only disaster can come of it." Warden

Alston assured the governor that he would "resolve the problem." How the warden planned to take care of the matter, or admit that there was any real issue that need to be resolved at all, was not made clear to the members of the baseball team.[9]

An article in the September 7, 1911, edition of the *Rawlins Republican* about the games the Wyoming Supply Company Juniors were set to play left many of the All Stars wondering when they would take the field next. Warden Alston announced the demise of the team at a prison meeting in mid-September 1911 and told his staff that teaching inmates how to read and write had to now be the main focus. Saban assured the ballplayers and the owners of local gambling dens that the decision was only temporary. He told owners of various saloons on Front Street in Rawlins that the emphasis on educating the convicts was only a ploy to draw attention away from the Death Row All Stars. "Once the excitement settles," Saban added, "the ball club will go back to doing what they do best."[10]

Local newspapers reported that offering inmates a primary education was an idea whose time had come. "Within the institution are many persons who were thrown upon their own resources at a very tender age and as a consequence their education is of a limited kind," an article in the October 19, 1911, edition of the *Wyoming Times* read. "And in some cases there has been no formal education at all." Large supplies of textbooks, tablets, and writing utensils were sent to the prison from schools around the state. Many prisoners anxiously looked forward to the chance to learn to read and write.[11]

Within two months' time talk of gambling on prison baseball had all but ended and insinuations of corruption on the part of Governor Carey and Warden Alston had been substituted with praise for bringing civility to the prison. The November 7, 1911, edition of the *Sheridan Post* boasted that by appointing Felix Alston as warden of the state penitentiary, Governor Carey had successfully made good on a primary campaign promise. "He [Governor Carey] told the people of Wyoming that he would uproot the lessee system with all its opportunity for graft," the article read, "and place the institution in the hands of the state, under competent upright and high-minded authority. The prison was completely renovated, new equipment added and the institution placed upon a business and humane basis.

"A very able man in the person of Felix Alston of Big Horn country was appointed warden to work out the plans of the state board. The present policy of humane treatment, heretofore unknown, and the firm discipline, have enabled the institution to turn out more and better work; and coupled with the substantial and wholesome food now furnished, prisoners are showing marked physical and mental improvements."[12]

In gratitude for the changes Warden Alston had made to the prison during his short time in the position, the inmates presented him with a Christmas gift. The gold pocket watch in a wooden case contained an inscription that read, "Presented to Felix Alston, Warden, by the Inmates of Wyoming State Penitentiary for his efforts on our behalf. December 25, 1911." The presentation was accompanied by a speech written on behalf of the prisoners by Rawlins citizen Charles E. Blydenburgh. "The conduct of such institutions as this has in the past in most of what is called the civilized world, been of such a character as to create and maintain a spirit of antagonism between the inmates and those placed over them, and they have been considered as places to carry into effect the vengeance of the law," Blydenburgh's speech began. "You coming as warden," he continued, "changed the spirit of management and the feeling between the inmates over them."[13]

The sentiment described by Blydenburgh was not shared by all the convicts, including members of Alston's baseball team. Upset that baseball games had been halted before the season had reached its natural conclusion, recalling the incentives given to teammates to win, and consumed with the idea that the warden was as corrupt and duplicitous as all the other administrators before him, one of the Death Row All Star members shared his opinions with the local newspaper. In the April 25, 1912, *Laramie Republican*, left fielder H. A. Pendergraft noted that "a great mistake had been perpetrated against the inmates of the institution" when Warden Alston was presented with a watch. "The facts of the matter may be summed up in their correct form," Pendergraft shared in his letter. "First, this collection was started by a few who carry their own currency and sleep in a feather bed compared to the rest of the inmates. Heralded during the campaign of 1910 as belonging to the dark ages of foreign corporations: It is worse today than under the old regime."[14]

Accolades heaped on Warden Alston and loyal supporters such as Governor Carey infuriated Otto Gramm. Although he had moved on professionally and politically, becoming director of the Laramie Lumber Company and Republican county committee chairman, he was bothered by the persistent talk that his dealings with the penitentiary had been less than honest. Plans to discredit Warden Alston's administration were thwarted when the All Stars stopped playing and wagers on the team and the players ceased as well. The fact that Joseph Seng's execution had been indefinitely postponed prompted Gramm to believe the ball club still had a future.[15]

Gramm decided to discuss the matter with Senator Warren. Allegations of malfeasance and a continued overall lack of discipline within the walls of the penitentiary were not news to the politician. According to articles in the *Carbon County Journal* and the *Rawlins Republican*, the practice of allowing prisoners to roam about the county as they pleased was still going on. Some inmates were now being allowed to take guns outside the prison and hunt for jackrabbits.[16]

If Senator Warren hoped to be in a position to restore order at the penitentiary, he would have to defeat Governor Carey in the 1912 election. With Gramm's considerable financial support behind him, Warren planned to challenge the governor's decision to make Felix Alston the warden and see to it that the death penalty was upheld for men such as Joseph Seng.[17]

Noted Wyoming attorneys Robert S. Spence and B. Rychman had managed to get a stay of execution for Seng while awaiting an appeal hearing. The case of Joseph Seng versus the State of Wyoming was taken under advisement by the state supreme court in mid-January 1912. In early April any hope Seng had for a reprieve was dashed when the judgment was affirmed. The court determined that "he must hang." Joseph's execution was fixed for May 24, 1912.[18]

On April 18, 1912, an article in the *Wyoming Tribune* announced that the gallows upon which Tom Horn, a lawman turned bounty hunter found guilty of shooting a teenage boy, was hanged in the Laramie county jail had been shipped to Rawlins to be used to hang Seng. "The state law now requires all executions to be in the state penitentiary," the article read, "and the gallows will doubtless remain there permanently."

Robert Spence informed Seng that there was one last option they could seek to save his life and that was Governor Carey. The governor could commute Seng's sentence to life in prison if he chose. Gramm suspected that to be the most likely scenario and wasn't shy about continuing to suggest the motivation for such an act would be to assure that the winning penitentiary baseball team remained intact.[19]

Anthony and Anna Seng asked their daughter Mary, a nun at the Franciscan Convent in Glenriddle, Pennsylvania, to pray for her brother. Several family members agreed to write letters to Governor Carey to ask for mercy. Among those writing letters requesting that Joseph's life be spared was Alta Lloyd. According to her family, Alta wrote more than one letter to the governor to ask that Seng's sentence be commuted. Those in her immediate sphere of influence in Wyoming believed nothing good could come from putting a man to death. "It won't undo what's been done," she reportedly told her friends the Ewers.[20]

According to the May 3, 1912, edition of the *Carbon County Journal*, numerous appeals to spare Joseph Seng's life were submitted to the governor, one of which was sent from Rev. J. Conrath of Rawlins. The reverend believed that Joseph shouldn't be hanged and asked the governor for a commutation of the sentence. "I ask your patience and kind consideration of the few words that I address to you in this letter," the clergyman began.

The key note of it lies in your proclamation of "Mother's Day", which I received lately and which reads very well.

The object of my words to you is to ask you to grant a favor on Mother's Day to a mother whom I know to be a true mother and worthy of great honor. It is the mother of Joseph Seng, who is sentenced to hang on May 24th. I would feel very guilty in the sight of God if I did not ask this favor of you.

Mrs. Seng is a mother of the true Christian type and a mother of twelve children, of whom her son Joseph proved to be a prodigal. This is no fault of hers and she loves him as a true mother. How many good mothers have not experienced the sadness brought on by a boy or girl that has wandered from their parental roof and been led astray. But who alone suffers? The mother. She is willing however to bear all except on things which must crush the life out

Joseph Seng's mother sent this picture to Governor Carey along with a letter pleading for her son's life. WYOMING STATE ARCHIVES, DEPT. OF STATE PARKS & CULTURAL RESOURCES

*of her and that is the thought that her son should meet death by the
gallows.*

*Seng's good people have often written their sad feelings to me.
They are poor and could give no financial assistance. They have been
buoyed up by the one hope that the sentence may be commuted to
life imprisonment. . . . There is one heart that is bearing it all, and
that is the heart of a sad mother who pleads to me for mercy for
her son. I feel crushed myself at the thought of it. I think to myself
what good is a corpse when life imprisonment is really the supreme
punishment? Death to Seng would be preferable to life imprisonment; were it not for his poor mother, who will surely die, he says,
if he must hang.*

*Let me plead with you to show your appreciation of a true
mother as expressed in your proclamation by using your authority
to save Seng from the gallows. What gratitude will come to you
from that good mother and family?*

*Regarding the case itself of Joseph Seng, I wish briefly to state
that I have not met a person who is acquainted with the case who
is in favor of capital punishment, for the reason that it was not
one-sided. Whether Seng is guilty or not of capital punishment is a
matter that does not enter into the substance of this letter, as I am
asking you this favor in behalf of the good mother who will suffer
with her family when Seng shall be a corpse.*

*I will be very grateful for the kindness you show to this good
mother and family, and I trust that my words may meet with your
favor.*[21]

Governor Carey responded to the correspondence on May 1, 1912.
"I have your letter of April 28 concerning the case of Joseph Seng, who
was convicted of murder," the governor replied. "I have not gone into

the Seng case as yet, as it has not been presented to me in a formal way. When it is I shall certainly give it consideration. Your letter shall be presented to the Board of Pardons if the matter comes up for consideration," the politician concluded.[22]

On May 11, 1912, a number of women in Rawlins followed Rev. Conrath's example and took up the matter of securing a commutation of the sentence of Joseph Seng. A petition to Governor Carey beseeching clemency on his part in the matter began circulating. The May 19, 1912, edition of the *Rawlins Republican* reported that practically every citizen in the city had signed it. According to the article, the ladies agreed that if Seng were guilty he should be punished for his crime, but they believed for his mother's sake his sentence should be changed to life in prison. "Seng has been a model prisoner while in the penitentiary," the report noted. "And those who have met him speak of him as an exceptionally fine man to have been guilty of the crime of which he is convicted. The universal sentiment seems to be that life imprisonment is sufficient punishment for him."

Rev. Conrath forwarded the petition and telegrams pleading for Seng's life to Rev. Masson in Allentown. According to the German-language newspaper the *Allentown Friedensbote*, "Reverend Masson was the only person Joseph confided everything. He wrote the spiritual advisor about playing baseball and offered that although his talent on the field might get him stays of execution it would not overturn a conviction. Rev. Masson encouraged him to offer the appellate court more of a reason to spare his life than a batting average. Seng wrote of the job he had with the railroad and mentioned that William Lloyd and others, objected to the way he "handled the hobos at the rail yard." Seng was emphatic that Lloyd tried to kill him when they crossed paths in the summer of 1910. Rev. Masson told a reporter at the *Allentown Friedensbote* that Joseph was "innocent." The June 4, 1912, edition of the paper noted that the reverend shared with them that Joseph's action was a "deed that occurred in self-defense."

Seng's version of the incident was also included in a later story about the accused in the August 12, 1919, edition of the German newspaper *Darmstädter Zeitung*. Seng confessed to the clergyman that on the evening of the alleged crime he witnessed William and Alta Lloyd arguing. "William had a strong grip on her upper arm and was leading her through the park. She was struggling to break free, but couldn't," he explained. "I tried to stop him and we ended up in a fight." The gun Joseph was carrying fell to the ground, and somewhere in the commotion that followed the gun was picked up and went off. The first bullet ripped through William's midsection and he dropped hard to his knees. Joseph was stunned and scrambled to his feet. That's when he saw Alta holding the smoking weapon. She was horrified. He pried the gun from her hands and tossed it aside. William was still alive and Alta was crying hysterically. According to Joseph's account relayed to Rev. Masson, he was so preoccupied with Alta's hysterics that he almost didn't see William pick up the gun and stand up. When he did notice, the gun was pointed at Alta. Joseph took the gun from William and shot him in the head.[23]

Alta was frantic. She hurried to her husband, dropped to her knees, and with the hem of her dress tried to stem the flow of blood pumping from the wound.[24]

Joseph Seng had never told the court this version of what had happened with William Lloyd the night he was killed. He made no attempt to alter the record even when he was assured of his fate.[25]

CHAPTER NINE

Seng at the Gallows

In the summer of 1911, the grass around the baseball diamond at the Wyoming State Penitentiary was a brilliant green. The slabs of canvas at home plate and at all three bases were faded white and dented by cleats that had tramped over them or slid into the sides. The walls surrounding the field were covered with scuff marks from fly balls and home runs. Ivy vines crawled along the stone backdrop in spots, breaking free to the other side.

By the summer of 1912, the outfield grounds were discolored and dominated by weeds. Only a handful of photographs existed to show that the Death Row All Stars had ever played there. Some of the pictures featured team members circling the bases after smacking the ball hard. "All baseball loves a hitter," a reporter at the *Wyoming Tribune* wrote about the game in April 1912. "The skill of a pitcher is rejected. The successful defensive work of infield and outfield, the one-handed stop or the running catch must ever arouse enthusiastic cheers; but when all is said and done, the wielder of the big stick is the giant that stirs the imagination and the hero worship of the fans.

"No thrill equals that which comes when a home player sends the ball ringing off his bat safely to the outfield. As the number of bases gained by such a hit increases, so does the excitement mount. When one of those drives wins a game, its maker is a hero—the fan can conjure no reward that is adequate. Those low in spirit whose countenance is lifted by such an achievement cannot fully express their appreciation for helping them to see, if only for a moment, beyond their despair."[1]

Professional baseball clubs like the Boston Rustlers and the St. Louis Browns, teams that ended the year of play with a 0.300 record or worse, could set their sights on improving when the 1912 season began. Not so with the All Stars. Once the ball club was disbanded in 1911, there would never again be a baseball team at the Wyoming State Penitentiary organized and managed by the warden. Inmates could gather players together for solitary games but would never again be allowed to compete outside the walls of the prison.[2]

By the time the 1912 baseball season rolled around, Warden Alston's thoughts were more on keeping order at the facility than playing the game. Prisoners were refusing to work, and many had been disobeying orders and had been placed in solitary confinement in the prison's dungeon. According to the May 8, 1912, edition of the *Wyoming Tribune*, Rawlins was thrown into a high state of excitement when ten convicts burrowed out of that dungeon. "The appearance of the men from the break in the dungeon wall at about 11 o'clock last night prompted the summoning of the guards," the article reported. "It resulted in the immediate capture of eight of the ten convicts. Two of the convicts, however, got over the prison wall and as of noon today have not been captured, although a posse was sent to scour the country immediately upon a count showing that two men were missing.

The baseball field where the Death Row All Stars once played has weathered with time. COURTESY OF AUTHOR

"While none of the convicts captured in the yard were armed and were placed in their cells without difficulty, it is believed that the men who got away must have had some assistance, as no trace has been obtainable of either of them."

Inmates who continued to be unhappy about the demise of the penitentiary baseball team and who were upset with what many convicts referred to as inhumane treatment and conditions at the prison wrote letters to Governor Carey asking that he "appoint an impartial non-political body of men to investigate the conditions at the prison."[3]

That spring and summer, Governor Carey was preoccupied with a variety of matters around the state, from encouraging voters to attend church services on Mother's Day to attending an oilmen's convention in Casper. He delivered speeches in Riverton and Cheyenne on a proposed irrigation system for parts of the region and campaigned for his son's (Robert D. Carey) run for Congress.[4] In between events the governor contemplated how to respond to the unrest at the penitentiary. His political and business adversaries, Senator Francis Warren and Otto Gramm, were aware of the issues at the prison as well. Both kept a watchful eye on the governor, ready to make public any errors in whatever decision he might make regarding the problem. Senator Warren was traveling throughout Wyoming, campaigning for reelection and explaining to his constituents that in spite of the news reports, he was not on board the *Titanic* when it sank.[5]

Gramm was also campaigning and hoping to get reelected to the office of Albany County secretary. Less than two years had passed since Governor Carey had removed Gramm as the head of the penitentiary's lessee program and forced his resignation from the Wyoming State University Board of Trustees. From the time of those events, Gramm had worked tirelessly to regain the confidence of voters, and he knew he could benefit at the polls if the governor and Warden Alston were not able to ensure the safety of the citizens by keeping inmates from escaping. A negative backlash could lead taxpayers to think Governor Carey's administration was corrupt and cause them to doubt the action he had taken against Gramm.[6]

Joseph Seng was scheduled to hang on May 24, 1912, and all stays of execution had been exhausted. Letters from family and friends had reached Governor Carey, desperately trying to persuade him to reconsider putting Joseph to death. Allowing Seng to live, however, would further fuel the rumors about gambling on the Death Row All Stars. Anna Seng, Joseph's mother, could not bear the thought of her son being led to the gallows. On May 12, 1912, she made one final attempt to get Governor Carey to change his mind about the harsh penalty set before Joseph. "Understanding this is mother's day which you instituted in Wyoming to honor the worthy mothers of the people of your state," Anna's telegram began, "I appeal to you to relieve my affliction by commuting the death sentence of my son to life imprisonment. I pray your honor to make at least one mother happy and will appreciate your clemency at the moment of my greatest distress. Mrs. Anna Seng."[7]

A letter from Joseph's younger brother Frank arrived at the governor's office the day after Anna's message. He, too, hoped to influence the governor's decision.

I am a boy twenty-three years old begging you for the life of my poor brother, whom I love as you love the members of your own family. A brother to whom I am indebted for a thousand and one kindnesses, Joseph Seng.

I do not know what the circumstances are surrounding the crime he committed, but I cannot believe that our Joe is bad enough for a fate like that. Governor, he has not a friend between Wyoming and Pennsylvania. Our family is a large one and we all have had to shift for ourselves. Poor Joe has made his own way since he was a little boy, and has never been a burden on his mother and father.

Our people are honorable, but we have no means. I am working for $15 a week and having my expenses to pay out of that I am not able to save much even to send to my mother at home. So that Joe has not had a cent to help him in his trouble.

Joe has never been called vicious; as I knew him he was anything else. I have not seen him now for six years. Won't you take into consideration, Governor that Joe made his own way since he was a mere child, with no one to train him, no one to direct him! Governor, save us this terrible ordeal! We have all had a hard life. We have never known the luxuries, and very few of the comforts, but our mother and father have tried, at least, to train us to be honest and straightforward.

There are twelve children in our family and this is THE FIRST CRIME THAT HAS BEEN LAID AT OUR DOOR. In God's Name, Governor, save us from this awful blow. Anything but the gallows as a heritage. We would not even be able to have his body sent home to Allentown, Pennsylvania.

I am enclosing mother's picture taken with one of her grandchildren. This is Joe's mother, Governor, and my mother. She is an upright Christian woman and this thing will KILL HER! Can you not for her sake modify the decree that will end her life in disgrace because one of the flock, who thinking it manly to go out into the world and earn his own way, has gone wrong?

Joe is not a degenerate, Governor! I do not know what the crime is but I would without knowledge say that it was committed *in the heat of passion or in defense of his life, for Joe, as I knew him, would not harm a kitten.*

Governor, in God's Name Save us! Hopefully, a prostrated brother, Frank Seng.[8]

Governor Carey responded to Anna on May 16, 1912. "Dear Madam," his letter began. "Your telegram has been received, and it together with all of the papers which have come to me, has been filed with the Board of Pardons for their consideration."

The Union Pacific Railroad carried the mail, including Governor Carey's response to Anna Seng, on an outgoing train in mid-May 1912. The vehicle made a regular stop in Evanston, Wyoming, before leaving the state for points east. Alta Lloyd had returned to the state in early May 1912 with her one-year-old child and was in Evanston awaiting the outcome of Joseph Seng's fate. According to her descendants, Joseph was the father of the child.[9]

After William Lloyd's death, Alta had traveled to Davenport, Iowa, where William's funeral was held on August 8, 1910. He was laid to rest at the Oakdale Cemetery beside his brother, who had passed away two weeks prior to William being shot. According to the August 5, 1910, edition of the *Davenport Democrat and Leader*, William's mother was "prostrated with grief over the double affliction that had fallen to her lot within a week."

William's obituary, along with the news of the incident leading to his death, was printed in the Davenport newspapers. The August 8, 1910, edition of the *Davenport Democrat and Leader* referred to William as "one of the best railroad detectives on the Union Pacific system. The unfortunate man was shot and killed by Joseph Seng, a former detective who three days previous had been discharged by Lloyd. On the evening of the shooting, Lloyd and his wife were approaching Mr.

Lloyd's private car when Seng approached them and after a few words drew his gun and fired three shots into the body of Lloyd. He then emptied the three remaining shots into the ground.

"Seng made no attempt to escape. He did not appear excited and told a bystander to inform an officer, warning others to keep away from him. Special city officer James Downs was soon on the grounds and Seng immediately gave himself up to the officer. Seng is reported to have made a very damaging statement previous to the shooting and it will prove premeditation on his part."

Alta had provided her own version of what happened the night William was killed to the editor of the Davenport newspaper the *Daily Times*. It was one of a handful of recorded instances she spoke of the event to the press. "She stated that on Thursday evening at 7 o'clock she and her husband were walking down near the railroad offices where Mr. Lloyd had been employed," the August 8, 1910, article read, "when they met a man by the name of Joe Seng. The trio stopped and conversed. Suddenly Mr. Lloyd turned to his wife and told Mr. Seng that he didn't wish to say anymore to him at that time. Mr. Lloyd and wife then resumed their journey, walking toward the railroad offices, Seng followed closely behind. Suddenly, Mr. Lloyd wheeled around evidently to say something, when Seng pulled the trigger."

Alta told the *Daily Times* reporter that William had a gun of his own, but that she didn't get a good look at it until it fell at his feet. According to Alta, the couple was on their way to the Leonard Amusement Co. Carnival when the altercation occurred. A large throng of people gathered on the scene moments after the shots were fired. William was transported to his railroad car, where he survived for thirty minutes before succumbing to the bullet wounds.[10]

The last legal execution held in Wyoming had been the hanging on November 29, 1903, in Cheyenne of Tom Horn, a bounty hunter found guilty for the murder of a young man named Willie Nickell.[11] In preparation for Seng's execution, construction workers at the penitentiary were restructuring the gallows that had last been used eight and a half years earlier. When Warden Alston wasn't dealing with numerous grievances from inmates and directing the state road contracts the convicts were honoring, he was overseeing the gallows project.[12] A new law dictated that executions should take place at the state penitentiary, and the builders were modifying the construction of the gallows to follow a newly designed system by which the condemned stepped on a platform and hanged themselves.[13]

The mechanics of the contraption, designed by architect James P. Julian, were arranged so that when the prisoner stepped onto the trapdoors, a plug was removed from a pail of water that acted as a counterbalance; when the pail was emptied, the trap would be sprung and the condemned would be dropped into eternity. Bags filled with sand, approximately Joseph Seng's weight, were used to test the mechanism. According to historians at the Wyoming State Penitentiary, it could take as long as thirty minutes for the counterweights to rise after the device was activated.[14]

On Thursday, May 23, 1912, final preparations were being made for Seng's execution. Barring any last-minute reprieve, Joseph was scheduled to be hanged at two forty-five the following morning at the penitentiary. Fearful of any uprising in the general population, Warden Alston ordered all inmates to be locked in their cells at noon on May 23. Alta Lloyd occupied much of Seng's thoughts in the last twenty-four hours of his incarceration. He confided to his spiritual advisor that "securing Alta's welfare and safety once and for always was his only interest."[15]

The *Wyoming Tribune* reported that Seng "seemed composed" while waiting for his life to come to an end. Prison guards assigned to watch over inmates on death row observed Seng calmly playing cards and drinking coffee. According to them, "he behaved as if his approaching death was the merest incident."[16]

News that the governor had decided not to interfere with the execution sentence didn't alter Seng's collected demeanor. He didn't seem surprised by the announcement, only resigned to his circumstances. He spent the last hours of his life staring sadly at a picture of his mother and writing letters to her and his siblings. While Seng was writing, a double quartet composed of prisoners sang hymns.[17]

Shortly after dinner on May 23, the Rev. Father Long of St. Mary's Cathedral in Cheyenne and Will Reid, editor of the *Carbon County Journal,* visited the condemned man. Seng spoke about the night William Lloyd was killed and stated that "many of the witnesses who testified against him told differently than what happened, while the witnesses who could have testified to the causes leading up to the shooting were not brought into the court room."

"The trouble which culminated in the shooting was not over the loss of his job," Reid later wrote that Joseph had told him. "Seng had tendered his resignation before he was discharged; but that it dated back to a quarrel which the men had some weeks before over a woman."[18]

"If I'd had a fair and impartial trial, and a lawyer who understood his business I never would have been convicted of murder in the first degree," Seng assured Reid at the conclusion of their talk.[19]

Just before two-thirty in the morning on May 24, Seng was escorted out of his cell by Warden Alston and the Rev. Father Long. A guard followed behind the trio as they began a slow walk to the gallows. "His steps were steady and he went to his death in a manner which stamped him as a brave man," the May 24, 1912, edition of the *Carbon County Journal* noted. "There was nothing of the braggadocio in his manner which was quiet and unassuming." A few spectators were waiting at the gallows when Joseph arrived. Among them were three doctors from the prison, Drs. Maghee, Adams, and Barber. Sheriffs and deputies from Carbon and Sweetwater Counties were there as well as a handful of Rawlins city officials.[20]

Seng stood before the dour-faced individuals at the event and smiled slightly. He was asked if he had any last words, and he nodded his head yes. After reiterating that he felt he did not have a fair trial, he told the onlookers that no one had ever given him a square deal except the warden and the penitentiary guards. Joseph then kissed Dr. Maghee and said, "Tell my mother good-bye for me, Doctor."[21]

Guards led Joseph up the stairs of the gallows to the platform ten feet above the ground. Immediately before him was the trapdoor. A black cap was placed over Joseph's head and a noose, hanging loosely from a beam overhead, was fashioned tightly around his neck. As soon as Joseph stepped on the trapdoor, a valve in a bucket of water hanging balanced with a small bag of sand opened. The running water caused the sandbag to drop, and as it fell it pulled out the bolt that held up the trapdoor Seng was standing on.[22]

According to the *Carbon County Journal*, Seng "fell five feet before he was jerked into eternity at the end of the rope." The falling of the sandbag, the rattling of the empty water bucket, the pulling of the bolt, and the crash of the doors as they dropped Seng's body through the trap that opened beneath him were the only sounds.[23] The fall did not break his neck, and he was slowly strangled. At 2:54 a.m., nine minutes and forty-five seconds after the trap was released, Dr. Maghee pronounced his former assistant dead. Seng's body was cut down, removed from the prison yard, and turned over to the county undertaker. The undertaker kindly agreed to furnish a casket and prepare the body to be shipped to Joseph's home in Pennsylvania.[24]

Julian Gallows, where Joseph Seng was hanged in May 1912. WYOMING STATE
ARCHIVES, DEPT. OF STATE PARKS & CULTURAL RESOURCES

Newspapers from Wyoming to Iowa carried the story of Seng's execution. The *Carbon County Journal*'s coverage included a letter written by Seng to those who had tried to help him while he was at the penitentiary. Given to Will Reid hours before Joseph was hanged, it read:

I am taking this means of expressing my gratitude and thanks to the people of Rawlins and vicinity for their kindness shown me in this my time and for the respect shown my mother and family in endeavoring to have my sentence commuted to life imprisonment.

I hold the greatest respect for those of you who tried. Although our combined efforts have been to no avail I know my mother will always look upon the people of Rawlins as friends and will always remember them in her prayers.

It is my desire to thank the prison authorities and especially Warden Alston for the favors and the kind consideration shown me during my confinement here, Mr. Reid for his efforts on my behalf through the columns of the Journal, Reverend Father Conrath and Father Long for their kindness and spiritual advice which has been a great comfort to me all through this ordeal, and especially Dr. Griffith Maghee who has shown me nothing but kindness and great cheer and has worked in an undying way to secure some consideration on my behalf. Oh, people you could not understand if I were to explain what a friend Dr. Maghee is to the unfortunate, not to me alone, but to all and everyone.

Again I thank each and every one of my friends who have tried to help me and also freely forgive my enemies. God bless you all. I am, Joseph Seng.[25]

On May 25, 1912, nearly four years after Seng had stepped off the train in Rawlins, he was on his way back to the town from whence he came. His body arrived in Allentown, Pennsylvania, on June 5 and he was buried the following day. Rev. Peter Masson conducted services in the Sacred Heart of Jesus Parish, and Joseph was laid to rest in the Holy Sepulchre Cemetery. Friends who had played baseball with Joseph when they were all boys served as pallbearers.[26]

CHAPTER TEN

The Last Inning

On Friday, May 24, 1912, Wyoming citizens awoke to the news that the execution of Joseph Seng had been carried out and that his body had been shipped to his aged mother. Below an article about the hanging posted on the front page of the *Wyoming Tribune* was a column announcing the scores of the National and American League baseball teams that had played the day before Joseph was put to death.[1] In stories that appeared about Seng's execution in newspapers as far away as Wellsville, New York, writers included a few sentences about how well the former inmate had played the game of baseball. Alston's All Stars never played again.

By the end of 1911, two of the infielders and two other players had served their time and been granted parole. Utility player Ora Carman's sentence expired on September 15, 1911, as did that of the left fielder Earl Stone.[2] Third baseman John Crottie was released in November 1911, and second baseman Frank Fitzgerald was released in December 1911. In 1912 several more players departed the prison. Left fielder

H. A. Pendergraft was granted parole in January 1912. Center fielder Sidney Potter's sentence concluded in June 1912, and so did that of pitcher Thomas Cameron. Cameron moved to Colorado and went to work as a coal miner. Shortstop Joseph Guzzardo was pardoned in July 1912 after helping to extinguish a fire at the penitentiary.

In early January 1913 team manager George Saban petitioned the State Board of Pardons for a reprieve, but his request was denied. Saban watched as Warden Alston's first baseman, Eugene Rowan, was granted parole in November 1913 and returned to his home in Rock Springs, Wyoming. On December 17, 1913, Saban escaped from the prison road gang he was working with near Manderson in Big Horn County.[3] According to the December 25, 1913, editions of the *Thermopolis Record* and the *Big Horn County Rustler*, Saban had help with his getaway. On January 16, 1914, the *Carbon County Journal* joined them in pointing out that Warden Alston had extended to him "all the privileges that any man serving a penitentiary sentence of twenty years could expect and then some." The *Journal* article continued:

> *D. O. Johnson, a special prison guard, was assigned to escort Saban back to the prison in Rawlins. Saban asked to be allowed to visit Basin to attend to business at the bank. This was granted, and he and Johnson stopped at a hotel. About 7 o'clock that evening Saban was allowed to go out and see some friends and that was the last seen of him.*
>
> *For some reason Johnson did not give the alarm until 11 o'clock the next morning, explaining his action by saying that he thought his man would return and that to report him would be to take away his credits.*
>
> *Saban seems to have evaporated. There are plenty of rumors but nothing authentic can be learned of his movements after leaving*

the hotel. It is said that an auto passed through Greybull [Wyoming] that night, but that might or might not mean anything. It is also said that his plan was to reach the coast and take passage for South America. There is another theory that he is hiding at the home of some friend in Basin.

All these stories are vague and may mean nothing. One thing is certain and that is that he ought to be easy to get if he is trying to make the getaway. The fact that he is a large man with a pleasant voice and manner, has a habit of smiling and showing a handsome set of teeth when he speaks, and has crippled hands ought to attract the attention of any officer who has his description. He is well-known through all this part of the country and unless he made a quick dash immediately on gaining his liberty he is pretty apt to run across someone who will know him.

It has been found out that Ora Allen, an associate of both D. O. Johnson and George Saban, left for Basin in his car the same night Saban escaped, with a mysterious passenger. They two were headed north. Allen was caught at Bridger, Montana, on the return trip from Laurel, where he had left Saban. We understand he admitted that he took the fugitive on the night flight, but claims that he thought all straight and right. The Journal reported that Montana authorities believed Allen and Johnson were working together to help Saban escape.

In support of his statement that Saban did not take a train at Laurel, Sheriff Orrick of Billings, Montana, quotes a conversation with an old friend of Saban's who saw and talked with the murderer at Bridger at the same time and when Allen was arrested the next day it was presumed Saban was in the neighborhood, as his sister and his mother reside on a ranch near Bridger.

"Wyoming officers after locating Allen apparently made no effort to locate Saban," said Sheriff Orrick, to all appearance accepting on face value his story to the effect that he left the escaped prisoner at Laurel. Later, according to Sheriff Orrick, Allen gave the lie to his plea of ignorance of the fact that Saban was supposed to be in custody by admitting he had Saban get out of the car and circle Greybull afoot in order that he might not be seen and recognized there where he is well-known.

Allen told the Wyoming officers he received $100 to take Saban across the line into Montana and said he believed Saban's statement that he was free. Johnson, the guard, said nothing of Saban's escape until the day after he disappeared.

"Montana officers made an effort to assist the Wyoming authorities to locate Saban until they discovered the Wyoming officers seeming indifference when they ceased their efforts," Sheriff Orrick declared. "The Wyoming authorities did not even visit the home of Saban's relatives to see if he had been there," he said."[4]

Ora Allen was eventually charged with unlawfully and feloniously assisting a convict to escape, and D. O. Johnson received a reprimand for being negligent. George Saban was never heard from again.[5]

To Otto Gramm, Johnson's involvement in Saban's escape confirmed his suspicions that the penitentiary administration was corrupt from top to bottom. He believed Warden Alston was ultimately responsible for Saban's getaway. In a letter to Senator Warren dated September 12, 1914, Gramm wrote that he "had no doubt that Felix Alston knew ahead of time that George would run. . . . He let him go when the threat of everyone finding out they were gambling on the inmate baseball team became too real for him."[6]

Epilogue

Three days after Joseph Seng was hanged, Governor Carey was in Riverton, Wyoming, discussing irrigation systems on the Wind River Reservation with the state land commissioner. Five months later he would travel to Rawlins to meet Felix Alston and local authorities to talk about the trouble at the penitentiary. The convicts were rioting. They had overpowered prison guards, and several prisoners had escaped. On October 14, 1912, Governor Carey sent troops to the area to suppress the battle between mutinous convicts and guards of the prison. "Eight convicts overpowered guards and escaped," an article in that day's edition of the Fond Du Lac, Wisconsin, newspaper the *Daily Commonwealth* reported. "One of those convicts, Lorenzo Paseo, who was serving a life term, was shot down, another, whose name is unknown, was killed by a posse of guards outside the prison. A third was mortally wounded. More than thirty escaped convicts are at large in the mountains around Rawlins, and practically every man in town is either fighting desperados or assisting in guarding the women and children of the city. The county for miles around Rawlins has been the scene of more fighting than at any time since the last Indian massacre."[1]

Although Wyoming citizens benefitted from the work that convicts did on various highways in the state, many were critical about the lack of strict supervision of the inmates. Warden Alston did not demand the level of security the prison population needed, both within the penitentiary and on work details outside the facility. Rawlins residents also felt that the inmates controlled too much of what went on inside the prison and that the warden was too busy to care about the issue and how it might adversely affect the community.[2]

A number of the state's law-abiding inhabitants believed that George Saban specifically ruled the prison population with Warden Alston's blessing. A report in the December 29, 1913, edition of the *Laramie Republican* illustrated that point and emphasized that a thorough investigation of Warden Alston needed to be done. "During the Big Horn County Fair at Basin during the fall, a man from southern Wyoming met George Saban on the street," the article noted. "What are you doing here, George?" asked the southern Wyoming man. "Just taking in the fair a little," responded the convict. The article continued:

"And it was literally the truth. From all accounts, it appears that George Saban, self-confessed murderer and presumed to have been under punishment for a term of twenty years, never has been treated as a criminal, but has had the best of everything, even personal liberties, to an exceedingly large extent.[3]

"He had not been in the penitentiary but a very short time before he was made a trustee. And the fact that he was going to picture shows and other places at Rawlins where convicts were not presumed to go called forth bitter demonstrations from people of Rawlins. When the road work came up Saban was sent out on that work and had had pretty much his way on the road gang. . . . The entire matter demands the closest scrutiny from the state authorities."

Less than a month after more than thirty inmates escaped and scattered from the penitentiary, two more broke loose from the dungeons of the building. According to the November 9, 1912, edition of the *Rawlins Republican*, "both escapees were rated among the meanest at the penitentiary and were always in trouble. . . . The general feeling of discontent at the penitentiary is due to the fact that all the men think they are being discriminated against because they were not chosen for the road gang."

The escapees were captured and returned to the Wyoming State Penitentiary, but confidence in the prison officials was shaken. State auditor Robert Forsyth openly expressed his concerns with the management of the penitentiary. In a letter to Governor Carey on the front page of the November 1, 1912, edition of the *Wyoming State Journal*, Forsyth called Warden Alston and his staff "criminal, incapable, insanely lenient, blind to reason and cautions. . . . I believe that the present condition of affairs at Rawlins to be without parallel in American prison history and that unless complete and sweeping reforms are at once instituted further and perhaps graver outrages, if such can be possible, will be perpetrated." Forsyth added, "As a citizen of Wyoming I deem it my duty to protest against the existing abuses and to demand a speedy correction of the same. As an official of the state, I will join you in inaugurating the proper reforms in the penitentiary, but unless such reforms are undertaken, you must take the responsibility for the continuation of the failure to properly administer penitentiary affairs."[4]

Alston rebounded from the controversy surrounding his first years as warden and remained in that position until March of 1919. During that time he conducted four more executions. The warden died in 1956 at the age of eighty-seven.[5]

Alta Lloyd moved to Pennsylvania in the summer of 1912. According to her great-niece, Alta's child died of pneumonia on

October 2, 1912. Alta committed suicide two days later. No one knows exactly where she is buried, but her family suspects she and her baby were laid to rest at the Sacred Heart Cemetery in Allentown. The cemetery plot records show that a body was buried in plot eighty on October 13, 1912, and lists that an infant is buried in plot eighty-two. Joseph Seng lies between Alta and the child, in plot eighty-one.[6]

Otto Gramm died on December 17, 1927, in Laramie, Wyoming, where he remained the principal owner and manager of the Laramie Coal Company.[7]

Governor Carey returned to the business of managing the state. His term ended in 1915. He passed away at his home in Cheyenne on February 5, 1924, at the age of seventy-nine, following a protracted illness.[8]

Senator Francis Warren died of pneumonia on November 24, 1929. Wyoming's senior senator had been in public office for thirty-seven years. "All walks of life bowed in humble solemnity as the sad news was heralded throughout the state and nation," the November 28, 1929, edition of the *Big Piney Examiner* reported. "His memory will forever stand in the hall of fame as a gallant hero, brilliant statesman, and a devoted citizen."

Senator Warren never had a friendly relationship with Governor Carey. They tolerated one another, but the senator remained suspect of Governor Carey and his politics until the day he died.[9]

The Julian Gallows, used to hang Joseph Seng, was retired in May 1933. A new form of execution, one the public and prison executives deemed "less barbaric and cumbersome," took its place. Lethal gas replaced the hangman's noose. In the summer of 1936, construction began on a gas chamber. It was built in the northwest portion of the prison hospital.[10]

In 1981, after serving the state for eighty years, the Wyoming State Penitentiary at Rawlins closed its doors. A new prison south of Rawlins was built, and the old prison became a historic landmark and museum.[11]

Notes

Introduction

1   *Indiana Gazette,* January 12, 2008; James, Historical Baseball Abstract, 7–9; Wild West, March 31, 2011.

2   *Wild West,* March 31, 2011; *Indiana Gazette,* January 12, 2008.

3   *Atlantic Evening News,* December 12, 1906.

4   McKelvey, *A History of Good Intentions*, 114–229.

5   Ibid.

Chapter One

1   *Farmers' Almanac Wyoming,* 1911; *Carbon County Journal,* August 4, 1911.

2   *Rawlins Republican,* December 14, 1911.

3   *Rawlins Republican,* July 20, 1911.

4   Individual prisoner intake forms, Wyoming State Penitentiary Rawlins; Brown, *Bad in the Good Old Days,* 37; Shillinger, *In Wyoming's Prison,* 197; "Felix Alston," Wyoming State Museum report, http://wyomuseum.state.wy.us/pdf/FelixAlston.pdf; Butler, *Gendered Justice,* 229–31.

5 Beard, *Wyoming from Territorial Days*, 4–15; Gould, *Wyoming from Territory to Statehood*, 11.

6 Klein, *Union Pacific*, 10–14; Larson, *History of Wyoming*, 36–41.

7 Gould, *Wyoming from Territory to Statehood*, 2–6; Klein, *Union Pacific*, 116–17.

8 Klein, *Union Pacific*, 103–4.

9 Ibid., 116–17.

10 Gould, *Wyoming from Territory to Statehood*, 108–11; Larson, *History of Wyoming*, 240–43.

11 *Cheyenne State Leader*, May 8, 1868; Gould, *Wyoming from Territory to Statehood*, 10–11.

12 *Cheyenne Daily Leader*, October 18, 1901; Shillinger, *In Wyoming's Prison*, X–XIV.

13 Larson, *History of Wyoming*, 230–31; *Time*, May 22, 1950; Wilson, *Outlaw Tales*, 131–33; "100 Years in the Wild West" photo supplement.

14 *Laramie Sentinel*, March 26, 1881; Wilson, *Outlaw Tales*, 131–33; Larson, *History of Wyoming*, 230–31.

15 *Cheyenne Daily Leader*, October 18, 1901; Shillinger, *In Wyoming's Prison*, X–XIV.

16 "100 Years in the Wild West" photo supplement; Larson, *History of Wyoming*, 145–48.

17 *Colorado Transcript*, December 16, 1896.

18 *Carbon County Journal*, December 14, 1901; "Board of Charities and Reform," http://doc.state.wy.us/about/charityreform.html.

19 *Salt Lake Tribune*, August 19, 1897; *Laramie Republican* Illustrated Section, 1915, 17.

20 Lichtenstein, *Twice the Word*, 3; Shillinger, *In Wyoming's Prison*, 47–52.

21 Lichtenstein, *Twice the Word*, 3; Shillinger, *In Wyoming's Prison*, 47–52; "Fast Facts about Broom Making at the Wyoming State Prison, Laramie," www.wyomingterritorialprison.com/wpcontent/uploads/2009/04/broomfactoryinterpguide.docx.

22 *Daily Tribune*, August 19, 1897; Shillinger, *In Wyoming's Prison*, 47–52; Butler, *Gendered Justice*, 229–31.

23 "Fast Facts about Broom Making."

24 *Laramie Republican*, June 23, 1911; *New York Times*, February 26, 1896; *Pacific Reporter*, May 19, 1898.

25 *Pacific Reporter*, May 19, 1898; *Daily Tribune*, August 19, 1897; Carey, Governor Executive Department Report; Shillinger, *In Wyoming's Prison*, 47–52.

26 "Fast Facts about Broom Making."

27 Shillinger, *In Wyoming's Prison*, 53.

28 Larson, *History of Wyoming*, 321.

29 Murray, *History of the Wyoming State Penitentiary*, 65–69.

30 *Laramie Daily Boomerang*, February 2, 2006.

31 *Laramie Republican*, April 25, 1912.

32 Shillinger, *In Wyoming's Prison*, 47–52.

33 Ibid., 17–20, 39–46.

34 Ibid., 47–52.

35 Carey, Joseph M. Governor Executive Department Report, Board of Charities & Reform Records, November 3, 1911.

36 *Bill Barlow's Budget*, April 19, 1911; Larson, *History of Wyoming*, 333.

37 Shillinger, In Wyoming's Prison, 69.

38 Larson, *History of Wyoming*, 321.

39 *Rawlins Republican*, October 14, 1912.

40 *Laramie Republican*, May 25, 1912.

41 Shillinger, *In Wyoming's Prison*, 85–88.

42 Alston, "Bronco Nell," 173–75.

43 Ibid.

44 Butler, *Gendered Justice*, 192–97; "Felix Alston," Wyoming State Museum report; Brown, *Bad in the Good Old Days*, 32–36.

45 *Rawlins Republican*, July 6, 1911; Larson, *History of Wyoming*, 207–208.

46 *Carbon County Journal*, June 2, 1911; *Carbon County Journal*, August 25, 1911; *Rawlins Republican*, May 19, 1911.

47 *Carbon County Journal*, July 24, 1911.

48 *Rawlins Republican*, August 10, 1911; *Rawlins Republican*, September 14, 1911.

49 *Carbon County Journal*, July 24, 1911.

Chapter Two

1 *Cheyenne Daily Leader*, April 8, 1909; Alston, ed., "The Spring Creek Raid, by Felix Alston," https://sites.google.com/a/wyo.gov/the–spring–creek–raid–by–felix–alston; Davis, "The Spring Creek Raid: The Last Murderous Sheep Raid in the Big Horn Basin," http://www.wyohistory.org/essays/spring–creek–raid.

2 *Laramie Daily Boomerang*, May 8, 1909; Alston, ed., "Spring Creek Raid"; Davis, "Last Murderous Sheep Raid in the Big Horn Basin."

3 *Grand Encampment Herald*, May 21, 1909; Alston, ed., "Spring Creek Raid."

4 *Grand Encampment Herald*, May 21, 1909; Davis, "Last Murderous Sheep Raid."

5 *Casper Press*, October 29, 1909; *Carbon County Journal*, May 1, 1909; *Basin Republican*, April 23, 1909.

6 *Casper Press*, October 29, 1909; Alston, ed., "Spring Creek Raid"; *Grand Encampment Herald*, May 21, 1909.

7 *Cheyenne Daily Leader,* April 8, 1909; *Powell Tribune,* May 10, 1909; Davis, "Last Murderous Sheep Raid."

8 *Casper Press,* October 29, 1909; *Grand Encampment Herald,* May 21, 1909; Davis, "Last Murderous Sheep Raid"; Alston, ed., "Spring Creek Raid."

9 Alston, ed., "Spring Creek Raid."

10 Ibid.

11 *Casper Press,* October 29, 1909; Alston, ed., "Spring Creek Raid"; Shillinger, *In Wyoming's Prison,* 221.

12 *Salt Lake Tribune,* November 17, 1907; National Association meeting minutes, February 19, 1907.

13 *Salt Lake Tribune,* November 17, 1907.

14 *Casper Press,* October 29, 1909; Alston, ed., "Spring Creek Raid."

15 *Anaconda Standard,* October 19, 1909.

16 *Cheyenne State Leader,* November 16, 1909; *Laramie Republican,* November 27, 1909; Davis, "Last Murderous Sheep Raid."

17 *Bill Barlow's Budget,* April 19, 1911; Bowen, *Progressive Men,* 737.

18 "Felix Alston," Wyoming State Museum report; Brown, *Bad in the Good Old Days,* 37.

19 *Wyoming State Journal,* April 21, 1911; Larson, *History of Wyoming,* 321; Farrington and Bakken, *Law in the West,* Civil Case 2514.

20 *Laramie Daily Boomerang,* June 19, 1903; Shillinger, *In Wyoming's Prison,* 48–50.

21 "Fast Facts about Broom Making at the Wyoming State Prison, Laramie," www.wyomingterritorialprison.com/wpcontent/uploads/2009/04/broomfactoryinterpguide.docx; Shillinger, *In Wyoming's Prison,* 53.

22 *Laramie Daily Boomerang,* August 5, 1911; Brown, *Bad in the Good Old Days,* 37.

23 Individual prisoner intake forms, Wyoming State Penitentiary Rawlins.

24 Davis, "Last Murderous Sheep Raid."

25 *Cheyenne State Leader*, July 11, 1911; *Sheridan Post*, August 8, 1911; Shillinger, *In Wyoming's Prison*, 147–49; *Wyoming Tribune*, August 11, 1911.

26 Baker, "Red Lights, Scarlet Women and Booze."

Chapter Three

1 Butler, *Gendered Justice*, 70; *Carbon County Journal*, August 18, 1911; Franscell, *Darkest Night*, 152.

2 Individual prisoner intake forms, Wyoming State Penitentiary Rawlins.

3 *Carbon County Journal*, August 18, 1911; Franscell, *Darkest Night*, 152.

4 *Allentown Morning Call*, September 14, 1931; Ancestry.com records for Joseph Seng; United States Federal Census, 1910.

5 *Allentown Morning Call*, September 14, 1931.

6 Allentown, Pennsylvania, City Directory, 1898; *Wyoming Press*, April 8, 1911.

7 *Allentown Morning Call*, September 14, 1931; Ancestry.com records for Joseph Seng; United States Federal Census, 1910.

8 Masson journal notes, September 1910–June 1915.

9 Ibid.

10 Baker, "Red Lights, Scarlet Women and Booze."

11 Masson journal notes.

12 Masson journal notes; Ancestry.com records for Moroni Ewer; United State Federal Census, 1910.

13 Klein, *Union Pacific*, 269–70; "Evanston Rail Yard," www.pwrr .org/prototype/Evanston/index.html.

14 *The Wyoming Press*, August 6, 1910.

15 *Casper Press*, June 7, 1910; Hallberg, ed., *Annals of Wyoming*, 78; *Big Piney Examiner*, August 1, 1918; Letter to WVD from Senator Francis Warren, April 20, 1906.

16 "CY Ranch," www.casperjournal.com/community/image_d070661d–673f–5cc3–9a95–2ce6957dfbb4.html.

17 *Carbon County Journal*, May 20, 1908.

18 *Journal*, June 13, 1908.

19 Klein, *Union Pacific*, 270; Masson journal notes.

20 E–mail exchange between Christopher Blue and Chris Enss, April 16, 2012.

21 Ibid.

22 *Daily Standard*, March 20, 1910.

23 *Standard Examiner*, February 23, 1922; *Laramie Republican*, August 6, 1910.

24 *Daily Standard*, August 6, 1910.

25 United States Federal Census, 1910.

26 E–mail exchanges between Olive Phelps and Chris Enss, November 19, 2011, April 12, 2012, March 2013.

27 E–mail exchanges between Olive Phelps and Chris Enss; *Rawlins Republican*, July 21, 1910.

28 E–mail exchanges between Olive Phelps and Chris Enss.

29 Ibid.

30 *Wyoming Press*, April 8, 1911.

31 Ibid., April 15, 1911.

Chapter Four

1 *Cheyenne State Leader*, September 14, 1910.

2 Masson journal notes, September 1910–June 1915.

3 Masson journal notes.

4   Ibid.
5   Individual prisoner intake forms, Wyoming State Penitentiary Rawlins.
6   Butler, *Gendered Justice,* 70; *Carbon County Journal,* August 18, 1911; Franscell, Darkest Night, 152.
7   *Big Horn County Rustler,* October 16, 1908.
8   *Laramie Republican Illustrated Section*, 1915.
9   *Laramie Republican,* June 23, 1911; *Nevada State Journal,* April 21, 1911.
10 *Carbon County Journal,* June 2, 1911.
11 Letter to Otto Gramm from Senator Francis Warren, August 1911.
12 *Bill Barlow's Budget,* April 19, 1911.
13 Larson, History of Wyoming, 632–33; Shillinger, *In Wyoming's Prison,* 66.
14 Shillinger, *In Wyoming's Prison,* 67; Gould, *Wyoming from Territory to Statehood,* 175–78.
15 Letter to Otto Gramm from Senator Francis Warren, August 1911.
16 Brown, *Bad in the Good Old Days,* 35–39.

Chapter Five

1   Baker, *"Red Lights, Scarlet Women and Booze."*
2   Shillinger, *In Wyoming's Prison,* 228–30.
3   *Laramie Republican,* July 18, 1911.
4   *Cheyenne State Leader,* April 19, 1911.
5   Carbon County Journal, July 22, 1911; *Rawlins Republican,* July 20, 1911.
6   *Farmers' Almanac Wyoming,* 1911; "Felix Alston," Wyoming State Museum report.

7   *Wyoming Press,* May 24, 1910; *Laramie Daily Boomerang,*
     September 18, 1909; *Cheyenne State Leader,* April 20, 1910; *Big
     Horn County Rustler,* April 14, 1911; *Natrona County Tribune,*
     August 13, 1911.
8   Warren Papers; Baker, "Red Lights, Scarlet Women and Booze."
9   *Carbon County Journal,* July 24, 1911.
10   Olson, "'I Felt Like,'" 176–79.
11   Reverend Peter Masson Journal Notes, September 1910–June 1915;
     Letter to Governor Carey from Mrs. Anthony Seng, July 1911.
12   *The Lehigh Register,* June 5, 1912.
13   *Carbon County Journal,* February 9, 1912; Olson, "'I Felt Like,'"
     176–79.
14   Olson, "'I Felt Like,'" 176–79; Shillinger, *In Wyoming's Prison,*
     197–98.
15   *Rawlins Republican,* May 8, 1920; "Felix Alston," Wyoming State
     Museum report.
16   *Big Horn County Rustler,* July 14, 1911; *Sheridan Post,* August 8,
     1911; *Cheyenne State Leader,* August 12, 1911.
17   *Carbon County Journal,* July 21, 1911; *Rawlins Republican,* July
     20, 1911; e-mail exchanges between Olive Phelps and Chris
     Enss, November 19, 2011, April 12, 2012, March 2013; Ancestry
     .com records for Moroni Ewer.
18   *Laramie Republican,* March 15, 1911; Masson journal notes,
     September 1910–June 1915; Masson journal notes; Baker, "Red
     Lights, Scarlet Women and Booze."
19   *Big Pine Examiner,* June 27, 1912.
20   Ibid.

Chapter Six
1   Olson, "'I Felt Like,'" 177–78.

2   Ibid.; Brown, *Bad in the Good Old Days*, 38–39.

3   Olson, "'I Felt Like,'" 177–78.

4   *Laramie Daily Boomerang*, August 5, 1911.

5   Ibid.

6   Individual prisoner intake forms, Wyoming State Penitentiary Rawlins; Masson journal notes, September 1910–June 1915.

7   Individual prisoner intake forms, Wyoming State Penitentiary Rawlins; Masson journal notes.

8   Masson journal notes.

9   Baker, "Red Lights, Scarlet Women and Booze."

10 Ibid.

11 Ibid.

12 *Guernsey Gazette*, August 4, 1911; *Basin Republican*, August 6, 1911.

13 Shillinger, *In Wyoming's Prison*, 86–89.

14 Cooley, "The Outdoor Treatment of Crime."

15 E–mail to Duane Shillinger from Scott Alston, February 2008.

16 Carbon County Journal, January 16, 1914.

17 *Laramie Republican*, June 23, 1911.

18 *Rawlins Republican*, November 21, 1908.

19 Ibid.; *Wyoming State Journal*, August 1, 1911.

20 Olson, "'I Felt Like,'" 177–78.

21 Ibid., 176–77.

22 Ibid.

23 Ibid.

24 Ibid.

25 Kinnaman, *Frontier Legacy*, 86–90.

26 *Cheyenne State Leader*, September 10, 1911.

27 *Rawlins Republican*, August 17, 1911.

Chapter Seven

1 *The Rawlins Republican,* April 14, 1910, and June 16, 1910.
2 "Felix Alston," Wyoming State Museum report.
3 Ibid.
4 *Rawlins Republican,* February 27, 1911; Meeting between Duane Shillinger and Chris Enss, July 26, 2013.
5 *Garland Guard,* December 9, 1905; *Thermopolis Record,* June 26, 1909, and August 11, 1910.
6 Baker, "Red Lights, Scarlet Women and Booze."
7 *Cheyenne Daily Leader,* December 27, 1907.
8 Masson journal notes, September 1910–June 1915.
9 *Laramie Daily Boomerang,* September 9, 1911; *Pacific Reporter,* May 19, 1898.
10 *Laramie Daily Boomerang,* September 26, 1911; *Laramie Republican,* August 21, 1911.
11 *Laramie Daily Boomerang,* June 9, 1911.
12 Letter to Governor Carey from Mrs. Anthony Seng, July 1911.
13 Ibid.
14 Letter to Mrs. Anthony Seng from Governor Carey, July 15, 1911.
15 Letter to Governor Carey from Rev. Peter Masson, July 12, 1911.
16 *Guernsey Gazette,* July 21, 1911.
17 *Rawlins Republican,* May 25, 1911; Masson journal notes.
18 *Cheyenne Daily Leader,* June 25, 1911.
19 *Carbon County Journal,* February 9, 1912; Olson, "'I Felt Like,'" 178–80.
20 *Pinedale Roundup,* October 17, 1912.
21 *Laramie Republican,* February 13, 1912.
22 Olson, "'I Felt Like,'" 173–75.

23 *Wyoming Tribune,* October 9, 1911; *Rawlins Republican,* May 25, 1911; Masson journal notes.

24 Olson, "'I Felt Like,'" 180–82.

25 Ibid.

26 Ibid.

27 *Rawlins Republican,* August 17, 1911.

28 *Laramie Republican,* August 25, 1911, and August 29, 1911.

29 *Laramie Republican,* March 20, 1912, and August 25, 1911.

30 *Rawlins Republican,* August 10, 1911; Kinnaman, "Frontier Legacy," 89–93.

31 *Wheatland World,* October 20, 1911; *Carbon County Journal,* October 13, 1911.

Chapter Eight

1 *Laramie Daily Boomerang,* November 6, 1911; *Rawlins Republican,* November 2, 1911; Shillinger, *In Wyoming's Prison,* 58–62; Brown, *Bad in the Good Old Days,* 38; *News Journal,* November 11, 1911.

2 *Laramie Daily Boomerang,* November 6, 1911; *Rawlins Republican,* November 2, 1911; Shillinger, *In Wyoming's Prison,* 58–62; Brown, *Bad in the Good Old Days,* 38; *News Journal,* November 11, 1911.

3 *Lander Eagle,* November 3, 1911.

4 *Laramie Daily Boomerang,* November 6, 1911; *Rawlins Republican,* November 2, 1911; Shillinger, *In Wyoming's Prison,* 58–62; Brown, *Bad in the Good Old Days,* 38; *News Journal,* November 11, 1911.

5 *Lander Eagle,* November 3, 1911.

6 *Cheyenne State Leader,* September 22, 1911,

7 Ibid.; Baker, "Red Lights, Scarlet Women and Booze."

8   *Park County Enterprise,* November 22, 1911.

9   E–mail to Duane Shillinger from Scott Alston, February 2008.

10 *Rawlins Republican,* September 7, 1911.

11 *Wyoming Times,* October 19, 1911; *Cowley Progress,* October 14, 1911.

12 *Sheridan Post,* November 7, 1911.

13 *Big Horn County Rustler,* January 5, 1912.

14 *Laramie Republican,* April 25, 1912.

15 Baker, "Red Lights, Scarlet Women and Booze."

16 *Cheyenne Daily Leader,* October 15, 1912.

17 Gould, *Wyoming from Territory to Statehood,* 166, 236.

18 *Wyoming Times,* December 28, 1916; *Cheyenne State Leader,* April 3, 1912; *Laramie Republican,* April 4, 1912.

19 *Wyoming Times,* December 28, 1916.

20 *Carbon County Journal,* May 3, 1912.

21 Ibid; Letter to Governor Carey from Rev. Joseph Conrath, April 28, 1912.

22 Letter to Rev. Joseph Conrath from Governor Carey, May 1, 1912.

23 *Darmstädter Zeitung,* August 12, 1919; *Rawlins Republican,* May 25, 1911; Masson journal notes, September 1910–June 1915.

24 Masson journal notes, September 1910–June 1915.

25 Ibid.

Chapter Nine

1   *Wyoming Tribune,* April 17, 1912.

2   James, *Historical Baseball Abstract,* 86–89; e-mail to Duane Shillinger from Scott Alston, February 2008.

3   *Pinedale Roundup,* May 2, 1912.

4   *Pinedale Roundup,* May 2, 1912; *Natrona County Tribune,* May 15, 1912.

5   *Laramie Daily Boomerang,* May 22, 1912; *Stockman Farmer,* May 21, 1912.

6   *Laramie Republican,* June 23, 1911; *Wyoming State Journal,* April 21, 1911.

7   Telegraph to Governor Carey from Mrs. Anna Seng, May 12, 1912.

8   Ibid.

9   E–mail exchanges between Olive Phelps and Chris Enss, November 19, 2011, April 12, 2012, March 2013.

10 *Daily Times,* August 8, 1910.

11 *Wyoming Derrick,* November 19, 1903.

12 *Wyoming Tribune,* May 21, 1912.

13 *Pinedale Roundup,* August 21, 1913; Wyoming Frontier Prison, www.wyomingfrontierprison.org.

14 *Pinedale Roundup,* August 21, 1913.

15 *Darmstädter Zeitung,* August 12, 1919.

16 *Wyoming Tribune,* May 24, 1912.

17 Ibid., May 23, 1912.

18 Ibid., May 24, 1912.

19 Ibid.

20 *Carbon County Journal,* May 24, 1912.

21 Ibid.

22 Ibid.

23 Ibid.

24 Ibid.; *Casper Press,* May 24, 1912.

25 *Wyoming Tribune,* May 24, 1912; *Evening Independent,* May 25, 1912.

26 *Lehigh Register,* June 5, 1912.

Chapter Ten

1   *Wyoming Tribune,* May 24, 1912.

2   *Cheyenne State Leader,* November 12, 1913; *Sheridan Enterprise,* July 30, 1912; *Cheyenne State Leader,* January 1, 1912; *Laramie Republican,* July 20, 1912.

3   *Thermopolis Record,* December 25, 1913; *Big Horn County Rustler,* December 25, 1913, and December 26, 1913.

4   *Carbon County Journal,* January 16, 1914.

5   Ibid.; *Thermopolis Record,* December 25, 1913; *Big Horn County Rustler,* December 25, 1913, and December 26, 1913.

6   Warren Papers.

Epilogue

1   *Riverton Republican,* May 31, 1912; *Daily Commonwealth,* October 14, 1912.

2   Shillinger, *In Wyoming's Prison,* 86.

3   *Laramie Republican,* December 29, 1913.

4   *Wyoming State Journal,* November 1, 1912; Shillinger, *In Wyoming's Prison,* 59.

5   "Felix Alston," Wyoming State Museum report.

6   E–mail exchanges between Olive Phelps and Chris Enss, November 19, 2011, April 12, 2012, March 2013; letter to Chris Enss from Rev. John Grabish, July 23, 2013; Seng, Charles F., tombstone Inscription at Holy Sepulchre Cemetery.

7   Civil Case Report #2514, *Law in the West,* Albany County Court.

8   *Pinedale Roundup,* February 28, 1924; Wyoming State Journal, November 1, 1912.

9   Warren Papers; *Laramie Republican,* December 26, 1913.

10 Wyoming Frontier Prison, www.wyomingfrontierprison.org.

11 Ibid.

BIBLIOGRAPHY

Books and Articles

Alston, Felix, with Scott Alston, ed. "Bronco Nell, a Woman Horse Thief." *Annals of Wyoming* 76, no. 4 (Autumn 2004).

Bakken, Gordon M., and Brenda Farrington, eds. *Law in the West*. Vol. 6 of *The American West*. New York: Garland, 2000.

Beard, Frances Birkhead. *Wyoming from Territorial Days to the Present*. Vol. 3. Chicago: American Historical Society, 1933.

Bowen, A. W. *Progressive Men of Wyoming*. Chicago: A. W. Bowen & Co., 1903.

Brown, Larry K. *Bad in the Good Old Days*. Worland, WY: High Plains Press, 1989.

Brown, Larry K. "Batter Up, Body Down," *True West* 49, no. 5 (July 2002).

Butler, Anne. *Gendered Justice in the American West: Women Prisoners in Men's Penitentiaries*. Urbana: University of Illinois Press, 1999.

Cooley, Harris R. "The Outdoor Treatment of Crime," *The Outlook*, February 1911.

Fink, Rev. Leo. "Four Diocesan Missioners of Christ," *Social Justice Review*, January/February 1968.

Franscell, Ron. *The Darkest Night: Two Sisters, a Brutal Murder, and Loss of Innocence*. New York: St. Martin's, 2007.

Gould, Lewis. *Wyoming from Territory to Statehood*. Worland, WY: High Plains Publishing, 1989.

Hallberg, Carl, ed. *Annals of Wyoming*. Cheyenne: Wyoming State Archives, 1880-2000.

James, Bill. *The Bill James Historical Baseball Abstract*. New York: Villard Books, 1988.

Kinnaman, William A. *Daniel C. Kinnaman, Frontier Legacy: The Story of a Genius and His Genes*. London: Lateral Thinkers International, 1992.

Klein, Maury. *Union Pacific: The Birth of a Railroad 1862–1893*. Garden City, NY: Doubleday & Co., 1987.

Larson, T. A. *History of Wyoming*. Lincoln: University of Nebraska Press, 1995.

Lichtenstien, Al. *Twice the Word of Free Labor: The Political Economy of Convict Labor in the New South*. New York: Verso Press, 1996.

McKelvy, Blake. *American Prisons: A History of Good Intentions*. Glen Ridge, NJ: Patterson Smith Press, 1993.

Murray, Robert A. *History of the Wyoming State Penitentiary at Rawlins*. Sheriden, WY: Western Interpretive Services, 1977.

Olson, Gordon L. "'I Felt Like I Must Be Entering . . . Another World': The Anonymous Memoirs of an Early Inmate of the Wyoming Penitentiary." Annals of Wyoming 47, no. 2 (Fall 1975): 153–90.

Reichler, Joseph. *The Baseball Encyclopedia*. New York: Macmillan, 1998.

Shillinger, Duane. *In Wyoming's Prison Hungry Men May Become Vicious Men*. Bloomington, IN: Authorhouse, 2004.

Shillinger, Duane. *Wyoming Attitudes . . . Short Ropes and Long Falls . . . Prison Walls.* Bloomington, IN: Authorhouse, 2002.

Wilson, Gary. *Outlaw Tales of Montana.* Guilford, CT: TwoDot, 2011.

Newspapers/Periodicals
Pacific Reporter
Time
Wild West
Ada (OK) Evening News
Allentown (PA) Friedensbote
Allentown (PA) Morning Call
Anaconda (MT) Standard
Atlanta (GA) Constitution
Atlantic (IA) Evening News
Bakersfield Californian
Basin Republican (Thermopolis, WY)
Big Horn County Rustler (Basin, WY)
Big Piney (WY) Examiner
Bill Barlow's Budget (Douglas County, WY)
Billings (MT) Gazette
Buffalo (WY) Bulletin
Carbon County Journal (Rawlins, WY)
Casper (WY) Press
Cheyenne (WY) Daily Leader
Cheyenne (WY) State Leader
City Sun (New York, NY)
Colorado Transcript
Coshocton (OH) Age
Cowley (WY) Progress

Daily Commonwealth (Fond Du Lac, WI)

Daily Globe (St. Paul, MN)

Daily Standard (Ogden, UT)

Daily Times (Davenport, IA)

Daily Tribune (Salt Lake, UT)

Darmstädter Zeitung (Darmstädt, Germany)

Davenport (IA) Democrat and Leader

Denver Post

Evening Independent (Massillon, OH)

Fort Wayne (IN) Daily News

Fort Wayne (IN) Sentinel

Galveston (TX) Daily News

Garland (WY) Guard

Grand Encampment (WY) Herald

Guernsey (WY) Gazette

Hutchinson (KS) News

Indiana (PA) Gazette

Journal (Westchester, NY)

Lander (WY) Eagle

Laramie Daily Boomerang

Laramie Republican

Laramie Sentinel

Lehigh Register (Allentown, PA)

Natrona County Tribune (Casper, WY)

Nevada State Journal

New York Herald

New York Times

News Journal (Newcastle, WY)

Park County Enterprise (Cody, WY)

Pinedale (WY) Roundup

Powell (WY) Tribune
Rawlins (WY) Republican
Reno (NV) Evening Gazette
Riverton (WY) Republican
Salt Lake (UT) Tribune
Sandusky (OH) Register
Sheridan (WY) Enterprise
Sheridan (WY) Post
Sioux County Herald (Orange City, IA)
Standard Examiner (Ogden, UT)
Stockman Farmer (Cheyenne, WY)
Sun News (New York, NY)
Thermopolis (WY) Record
Washington Post
Waterloo (IA) Evening Courier
Wellsville (NY) Daily Reporter
Wheatland (WY) World
Wind River Mountaineer (Lander, WY)
Wyoming Derrick (Casper)
Wyoming Press (Evanston)
Wyoming State Journal (Lander)
Wyoming Times (Evanston)
Wyoming Tribune (Cheyenne)

Websites

Alston, Felix Scott, ed. "The Spring Creek Raid, by Felix Alston," https://sites.google.com/a/wyo.gov/the-spring-creek-raid-by-felix-alston.

Ancestry.com records for Felix Alston, Joseph Carey, Moroni Ewer, and Joseph Seng.

"Board of Charities and Reform," Wyoming Department of Corrections, http://corrections.wy.gov/about/charityreform.html.

"Convict Lease System," Wyoming Department of Corrections, http://corrections.wy.gov/about/charityreform.html.

"CY Ranch," Casper Journal, www.casperjournal.com/community/image_d070661d-673f-5cc3-9a95-2ce6957dfbb4.html.

Davis, John W. "The Spring Creek Raid: The Last Murderous Sheep Raid in the Big Horn Basin," Wyoming State Historical Society, www.wyohistory.org/essays/spring-creek-raid.

"Evanston Rail Yard," Piedmont and Western Railroad Club, www.pwrr.org/prototype/Evanston/index.html.

"Evolution of Gambling in the United States: Wild West Saloons," www.casinosevolution.com/american-gambling-history.htm.

"Fast Facts about Broom Making at the Wyoming State Prison, Laramie," www.wyomingterritorialprison.com/wp-content/uploads/2009/04/broomfactoryinterpguide.docx.

"Felix Alston (1869–1956)," Wyoming State Museum report, http://wyomuseum.state.wy.us/pdf/FelixAlston.pdf.

"Monsignor Peter Masson," Pennsylvania Biographies, www.historicpa.net/bios/2p/peter-masson-mon.html.

"Overview of the Wyoming Court System/Wyoming Judicial Branch," www.courts.state.wy.us/wyomingjudicialbranch.org.

Union Pacific Railroad, www.up.com.

"Western Regional Railroads," www.r2parks.net/West.html.

Wyoming Frontier Prison, www.wyomingfrontierprison.org.

Wyoming State Penitentiary, http://corrections.wy.gov/institutions/wsp/index.html.

Correspondence

Letter to WVD from Senator Francis Warren, April 20, 1906.

Letter to Otto Gramm from Senator Francis Warren, August 1911.

Letter to Governor Carey from Mrs. Anthony Seng, July 1911.

Letter to Governor Carey from Rev. Peter Masson, July 12, 1911.

Letter to Mrs. Anthony Seng from Governor Carey, July 15, 1911.

Letter to Rev. Peter Masson from Governor Carey, July 15, 1911.

Letter to Governor Carey from Rev. Joseph Conrath, April 28, 1912.

Letter to Rev. Joseph Conrath from Governor Carey, May 1, 1912.

Letter to Governor Carey from Frank Seng, May 13, 1912.

Letter to Anna Seng from Governor Carey, May 16, 1912.

Telegraph to Governor Carey from Mrs. Hayes, Mrs. Ivy, and Mrs. Quinn, May 11, 1912.

Telegraph to Governor Carey from Mrs. Anna Seng, May 12, 1912.

Telegraph to Governor Carey from Rev. Peter Masson, May 20, 1912.

Telegraph to Governor Carey from Sister M. Bonaventura Seng, May 21, 1912.

E-mail to Duane Shillinger from Scott Alston, February 2008.

E-mail exchanges between Chris Enss and Olive Phelps, relative of Alta Lloyd, November 19, 2011; April 12, 2012; March 2013.

E-mail exchange between Chris Enss and Charles F. Seng, relative of Joseph Seng, September 2012.

E-mail exchange between Chris Enss and Rev. John Grabish, spiritual advisor to Joseph Seng, July 24, 2013.

E-mail exchange between Chris Enss and Christopher Blue, outreach assistant at Union Pacific Railroad Museum, April 16, 2012.

Letter to Chris Enss from Rev. John Grabish, Minister at Sacred Heart Church in Allentown, Pennsylvania, July 23, 2013.

Meeting between historian Duane Shillinger and Chris Enss, July 26, 2013.

Miscellaneous

"100 Years in the Wild West: A Pictorial History of Rawlins, Wyoming." Supplement to the *Daily Times*, 1968.

Allentown, Pennsylvania, City Directory, 1898.

Baker, Rans. "Red Lights, Scarlet Women and Booze: Rawlins Red Light Districts." Research report for Rawlins Historical Society, no year given.

Carey, Joseph M. *Governor Executive Department Report: Board of Charities and Reform Records*, November 21, 1911.

Christmas speech and gift for Warden Alston presented by Charles E. Bydenburgh, December 25, 1911.

Farmers' Almanac Wyoming, 1911.

Individual prisoner intake forms, Wyoming State Penitentiary, Rawlins, 1910–11.

J-A-B-S Wyoming State Penitentiary inmate newsletter: June 1911; July 4, 1914; March 1916; May 1916; June 1916; February 1917.

Kearny, Nebraska, City Directory, 1908.

Laramie Republican Illustrated Section, 1915.

National Association of Wool Growers meeting minutes, February 19, 1907.

Masson, Reverend Peter, journal notes, September 1910–June 1915.

Rawlins, Wyoming, City Directory, August 1907.

Seng, Charles F., tombstone inscription at Sacred Heart Cemetery (formerly Holy Sepulchre Cemetery), Allentown, Pennsylvania, 1968.

State v. Gramm, in *Wyoming Reports: Cases Decided in the Supreme Courts of Wyoming*. Vol. 7. Laramie, WY: Prairie Press, 1900.

US Department of Commerce and Labor, Bureau of the Census. Thirteenth Census of the United States, 1910 Population.

Warren Papers. Material from Senator Francis Warren's files at the University of Wyoming, Laramie.

Wyoming State Business Directory, 1910.

Index

ABOUT THE AUTHORS

Howard Kazanjian is an author and award-winning producer and entertainment executive who has been producing feature films and television programs for more than twenty-five years. While vice president of production for Lucasfilm Ltd., he produced two of the highest-grossing films of all time: *Raiders of the Lost Ark* and *Star Wars: Return of the Jedi.* He also managed production of another top-ten box office hit, *The Empire Strikes Back.* Some of his other notable credits include *The Rookies, Demolition Man,* and the two-hour pilot and first season of *JAG.*

Chris Enss is a *New York Times* best-selling author and an award-winning screenwriter who has written for television, short subject films, live performances, and the movies. She is the coauthor or author of more than twenty-five books, including *The Cowboy and the Senorita, Happy Trails, The Young Duke,* and *Thunder Over the Prairie*—soon to be a motion picture—with Howard Kazanjian. Her recent books include *Frontier Teachers: Stories of Heroic Women of the Old West* and

The Doctor Wore Petticoats. Enss has done everything from stand-up comedy to working as a stunt person at the Old Tucson Movie Studio. She learned the basics of writing for film and television at the University of Arizona.